Bible Interpretations

Sixteenth Series
April 7 - June 30, 1895

Mark, Luke & John

Bible
Interpretations
Sixteenth Series
Mark, Luke & John

These Bible Interpretations were published in the Inter-Ocean Newspaper in Chicago, Illinois, during the late 1890's.

By
Emma Curtis Hopkins

President of the Emma Curtis Hopkins Theological Seminary at Chicago, Illinois

WISEWOMAN PRESS

Bible Interpretations: Sixteenth Series

By Emma Curtis Hopkins

© WiseWoman Press 2013

Managing Editor: Michael Terranova

ISBN: 978-0945385-67-7

WiseWoman Press

Vancouver, WA 98665

www.wisewomanpress.com

www.emmacurtishopkins.com

CONTENTS

Editor's Note

All lessons starting with the Seventh Series of Bible Interpretations are Sunday postings from the Inter-Ocean Newspaper in Chicago, Illinois. Many of the lessons in the following series were retrieved from the International New Thought Association Archives in Mesa, Arizona, by Rev. Joanna Rogers. Others were retrieved from libraries in Chicago, and the Library of Congress, by Rev. Natalie Jean.

All the lessons follow the Sunday School Lesson Plan published in "Peloubet's International Sunday School Lessons." The passages to be studied are selected by an International Committee of traditional Bible Scholars.

Some of Emma's lessons don't have a title. In these cases the heading will say "Comments and Explanations of the Golden Text," followed by the Bible passages to be studied.

Foreword

By Rev. Natalie R. Jean

I have read many teachings by Emma Curtis Hopkins, but the teachings that touch the very essence of my soul are her Bible Interpretations. There are many books written on the teachings of the Bible, but none can touch the surface of the true messages more than these Bible interpretations. With each word you can feel and see how Spirit spoke through Emma. The mystical interpretations take you on a wonderful journey to Self Realization.

Each passage opens your consciousness to a new awareness of the realities of life. The illusions of life seem to disappear through each interpretation. Emma teaches that we are the key that unlocks the doorway to the light that shines within. She incorporates ideals of other religions into her teachings, in order to understand the commonalities, so that there is a complete understanding of our Oneness. Emma opens our eyes and mind to a better today and exciting future.

Emma Curtis Hopkins, one of the Founders of New Thought, teaches us to love ourselves, to speak our Truth, and to focus on our Good. My life has moved in wonderful directions because of her teachings. I know the only thing that can move me in this world is God. May these interpretations guide you to a similar path and may you truly remember that "There Is Good For You and You Ought to Have It."

Introduction

Emma Curtis Hopkins was born in 1849, in Killingsly, Connecticut. She passed on April 8, 1925. Mrs. Hopkins had a marvelous education and could read many of the world's classical texts in their original language. During her extensive studies she was always able to discover the Universal Truths in each of the world's sacred traditions. She quotes from many of these teachings in her writings. As she was a very private person, we know little about her personal life. What we do know has been gleaned from other people or from the archived writings we have been able to discover.

Emma Curtis Hopkins was one of the greatest influences on the New Thought movement in the United States. She taught over 50,000 people the Universal Truth of knowing "God is All there is." She taught many of the founders of early New Thought, and in turn these individuals expanded the influence of her teachings. All of her writings encourage the student to enter into a personal relationship with God. She presses us to deny anything except the Truth of this spiritual Presence in every area of our lives. This is the central focus of all her teachings.

The first six series of Bible Interpretations were presented at her seminary in Chicago, Illinois. The remaining Series, probably close to thirty, were printed in the Inter Ocean Newspaper in Chicago. Many of the lessons are no longer available for various reasons. It is the intention of WiseWoman Press to publish as many of these Bible Interpretations as possible. Our hope is that any missing lessons will be found or directed to us.

I am very honored to join the long line of people that have been involved in publishing Emma Curtis Hopkins's Bible Interpretations. Some confusion exists as to the numbering sequence of the lessons. In the early 1920's many of the lessons were published by the Highwatch Fellowship. Inadvertently the first two lessons were omitted from the numbering system. Rev. Joanna Rogers has corrected this mistake by finding the first two lessons and restoring them to their rightful place. Rev. Rogers has been able to find many of the missing lessons at the International New Thought Alliance archives in Mesa, Arizona. Rev. Rogers painstakingly scoured the archives for the missing lessons as well as for Mrs. Hopkins's other works. She has published much of what was discovered. WiseWoman Press is now publishing the correctly numbered series of the Bible Interpretations.

In the early 1940's, there was a resurgence of interest in Emma's works. At that time, Highwatch Fellowship began to publish many of her writings, and it was then that *High Mysticism,* her seminal work was published. Previously, the material contained in High Mysticism was only available as individual lessons and was brought together in book form at that time. Although there were many errors in these first publications and many Bible verses were incorrectly quoted, I am happy to announce that WiseWoman Press is now publishing *High Mysticism* in 'the correct format'. This corrected form was scanned faithfully from the original, individual lessons.

The next person to publish some of the Bible Lessons was Rev. Marge Flotron of the Ministry of Truth International in Chicago, Illinois. She published Bible Lessons as well as many of Emma's other works. By her initiative, Emma's writings were brought to a larger audience when DeVorss & Company, a longtime publisher of Truth teachings, took on the publication of Ms. Hopkins' key works.

In addition, Dr. Carmelita Trowbridge, founding minister of The Sanctuary of Truth in Alhambra, California, inspired her assistant minister, Rev. Shirley Lawrence, to publish many of Emma's works, including the first three series of Bible Interpretations. Rev. Lawrence created mail order courses for many of these Series. She has graciously passed on any information she had, in order to assure that these works continue to inspire individuals and groups who are called to further study of the teachings of Mrs. Hopkins.

Finally, a very special acknowledgement goes to Rev. Natalie Jean, who has worked diligently to retrieve several of Emma's lessons from the Library of Congress, as well as libraries in Chicago. Rev. Jean hand-typed many of the lessons she found on microfilm. Much of what she found is on her website, www.highwatch.net.

It is with a grateful heart that I am able to pass on these wonderful teachings. I have been studying dear Emma's works for fifteen years. I was introduced to her writings by my mentor and teacher, Rev. Marcia Sutton. I have been overjoyed with the results of delving deeply into these Truth Teachings.

In 2004, I wrote a Sacred Covenant entitled "Resurrecting Emma," and created a website, www.emmacurtishopkins.com. The result of creating this covenant and website has brought many of Emma's works into my hands and has deepened my faith in God. As a result of my love for these works, I was led to become a member of Wise-Woman Press and to publish these wonderful teachings. God is Good.

My understanding of Truth from these divinely inspired teachings keeps bringing great Joy, Freedom, and Peace to my life.

Dear reader; It is with an open heart that I offer these works to you, and I know they will touch you as they have touched me. Together we are living in the Truth that God is truly present, and living for and through each of us.

The greatest Truth Emma presented to us is "My Good is my God, Omnipresent, Omnipotent and Omniscient."

Rev. Michael Terranova

WiseWoman Press

Vancouver, Washington, 2010

—

LESSON I

The Triumphal Entry

Mark 11:1-11

This lesson illustrates the self-authorizing effect of great principles carefully looked after. Presently, they imbue their votaries with their own energy. If they are changeless fact, they give a reliable character to an unstable mind. As Bonaparte set the crown of empire on his own head inspired by the principle of conquest by guns, (as that idea had been spreading itself) and found his crown but a temporary glory, so Jesus set the crown of empire on His own head inspired by the principle of conquest by peace as that eternal presence was known by him, and "of His Kingdom there shall be no end."

The idea of gaining what is my right by sabering and shooting, quarreling and protesting, is a pro-tem wisp flourishing itself on the face of God. If what is mine cannot come to me drawn by the divine lode-star within me I shall find all that comes by my setting my heel on the homes and footholds of my fellowmen but a thorny pillow, a disquieting bauble. Because that principle of setting down heels is an assumption of mortal mind, therefore it has no substance in it. While the lodestar's mighty conquests by everlasting principle, bruising no hearts, blasting no homes, defrauding no lives, so they march in their stately majesty toward me, shall be my rest and my activity, one and the same, my simplicity and my majesty, inseparable unity, my yielding and my authority undivided in greatness. One is the Bonaparte principle, which is nothing. The other is the Jesus principle, which is substance.

There is no doubt whatever but that there are certain greatness, certain goods, certain knowledge, which are each man's particular rights. Those properties would reach him anyway if he were giving heed to the exposure of the divine lode-star that shines all by itself in his heart covered by the veils of make-shifts. He needs no hand-to-hand conflict with man or nature to bring them his way.

Archimedes followed mathematical relations. They taught him their secret of fearlessness. At the taking of Syracuse the soldiers thrust their sabers forward to run him through. "*Noli turbare circulos meos,*" (Do not disturb my circles) was all he said. Whosoever is following after that which cannot die is himself unkillable. Whoever is following after the Shining One, he himself has unassailable majesty.

Jesus of Nazareth knew about this. Who taught Him that to be king of Rome and ruler of the Jews by Pompey's highly praised system would be an insult to the lode-star of divinity within Him, no book telleth us. But He knew it. Millions of people stood ready to call out soldiers to cut off heads and plunder palaces for His sake, but what the lode-star drew out He would not have. The Greeks offered him the leadership of their philosophical institutes, but what cause but their recognition of the divine facts He brought to light He would not have.

"No man cometh unto me save the Father that is in me draw him."

"Glorify me, Father."

Idle Boasts Which Have No Foundation

We boast of the printing press, the commerce, the railroading, and manufacturing that sprang up under the Christian dispensation. They have had no Christian dispensation in them; they have not been run on Christian plans nor used for Christian purposes. But they have come up side by side with the acknowledgements of the Christian principle as the one absolute fact in the universe.

Even the one-sided assertion that Jesus was all divine, has illustrating and energizing force about it. Calling Gautama divine and practicing against him has bred child widows. Calling Jesus divine and doing not his way has built railroads. But actually taking these two men at their word and letting the practice into oblivion and dividing up the money of the syndicates equally dollar for dollar with all who helped build the railroads and sail the ships and print the books and erect their factories, not a rich man would be left, and not a poor man would be left. The spirit of share and share alike would animate the globe. The spirit of the equal rights of all alike to all the privileges and opportunities and goods of heaven and earth would animate the world. There would be no learned. There would be no unlearned. There would be no employed. There would be no employer. For these are all anti-Christian.

Did not Jesus Christ teach that by wholly acknowledging the principle of which He forever would be a living embodiment, men should know everything without books? Did He not teach that by attending to the same mighty One of whom He Himself was the living word, all men would live forever and no accidents would ever happen unto them? Did he not teach that by agreeing with Him, disease would never be heard of? Did He not insist that mankind might all show that they were all God and nothing else right here and now on this planet, not waiting to go anywhere or be absorbed into anything? Did he not show by His own exposures of power that all men were by original birth kings and magi?

Today's lesson takes one of His ways of exhibiting how all owners of animals do truly act when a man knows his own original spirit. They are eager to lend them. They charge nothing. It shows how eagerly the world builds free highways, piling them softly with plush and wool and linen that the dust may not spoil His white raiment, nor the sound of hoofs jar on the hosannas of the children who chant glad welcome.

The Life Journey of Jesus of Nazareth

Just what opens the rock hearts of this world, and just what caused the children in the factories of civilization to sing, and just what makes all men eager to do everything freely? Today's lesson tells. While my coat is trembling with fingers of children in the stockyards, in the stores, in the arctic waters, let me never dare lisp that it is a Christian coat. While I pay my fare on the railroads, and charge money for my healing ministry, that I may pay my rents and buy my books, let me not say aloud that I boast of having entered into the principle lived by Jesus of Nazareth as announced in this lesson Mark 11:1-11.

Every action of the life's journey of Jesus of Nazareth gives one result of living by attention to the Original Spirit, which hath its abode in all men alike. This lesson takes up the subject of spontaneous mutual service and free riding and sailing, wherever one wants to go who goeth in the mystic potentiality of his self-knowledge.

Whoever knows his own kingship, and accepts it goes free, is clothed free of charge, is fed without cost. This is the privilege of all men alike. They are all divine.

5

Therefore they all serve and offer and bestow and give like kings divine. The office of king was originally the office of ministering largely, magnificently, royally, kindly. In the days when it degenerates into bleeding with taxes and doing nothing but dress up to walk through forms, the people learn to look away from the symbol to the fact, and that fact is the glorious potency of their own actual spirit.

It is good for the world when its rulers play at fools. That time is now. Therefore now it is good to live, for there are no personal examples, and the world must look from the fading forms to the Eternal Presence.

"Jerusalem" is a word that stands for native kingship. It means the actual estate of the organ-grinder man with no legs. It is my native nature. It is your native nature. The golden home of the king in his shining glory. Now it is written that "when they come nigh to Jerusalem unto Bethphage and Bethany, at the Mount of Olives, He sendeth forth two of his disciples."

This sentence shows how we act as we draw nigh to the lode-star of the God in our bosom. We send forth two qualities, Peter and John, transformed from their worldly methods to their divine efficiencies. Peter is that power of formulating our words, which we all exercise foolishly as we speak on the negative, or wisely as we speak on the positive concerning ourselves.

The Jerusalem Center of Self

Emerson proclaimed that whom the gods called to greatness they overloaded with disadvantages. This was an assertion on the negative side of life. He formulated these words into some immense disadvantage for himself. The Shunamite woman had been better taught than that. She spoke on the positive side of life when she said, "it is well."

Nigh the Jerusalem center of ourselves we say wonderful things that are true and they formulate quickly. Bethphage is figs, for the plenty, bounty, rich provisions everywhere. He who is looking toward the lode-star, the Jerusalem of himself, formulates provisions without waiting to employ gardeners and husbandmen. There are better ways of being fed on this journey of life quite different from the digging and hoeing plans in vogue.

John is that power of doing more than as have mentioned by the words of our mouth or the meditations of our hearts. It is free grace whereby the mountains and the hills let out their secrets that we never spoke of.

The thief asked for a little thought of him in his anguish, and lo! He was lifted into Paradise. The three kings asked Elisha for water and got all the cities of the Moabites. Lincoln asked for the freedom of the Southern slaves and liberated all the serfs of Russia. The John quality of the organ-grinder gets more misery than he bargained for on the outward bound trip of his dealing with his life, but doubles and triples his blessings on the homeward-bound trip of his mind. The main thing to speak of is Jerusalem. The only place to steer for is Jerusalem. We touch Bethphage, bounty of our word, as we look hitherward. We touch Bethany, house of dates, more than we can possibly use above any word we have spoken or thought we have thought on our journey toward the lode-star of home. This is truth. The triumphal entry into Jerusalem was intended to stand as a segment by itself to illustrate the signals that fly from the battlements of the promontories of human provisions that are made for every man headed outward. And no other kind of provisions is honestly Christian.

Returning Memories of Paradise

The multitude bore around the Mount of Olives. So he who strikes for the soul that shines in his own bosom catches the spicy flavors of intelligence altogether new. He feels a quaint wisdom dawning on his heart. There's no hour breaking when ye shall know what the schools cannot remember. The tender grace of spiritual knowledge comes from the mountain heights that gleam with the eternal light of the Jerusalem of being. It is the spicy memory returning, memory of the land from which we all hailed. There is no ignorance there. There is nothing too hard for us there. Olivet stands for returning memories of Paradise; its name is Jerusalem in this segment. Sometimes it is knowledge. Sometimes it is Jesus Christ. But not one of these names is the real name. That is unspeakable by lips that use the language of earth.

And note how the young beast stood waiting to hear the Man who took the kingship belonging to Him, and note how the children sang and people spread perfumed palms and soft carpets in his way because He Himself knew that He was King. The winds know that the organ grinder and the car conductor and the typesetter are kings. The stars know it. The stones laugh under their feet, whispering about the royal sandals that belong to them and the songs of the children who would sing in their ears if they would head for Jerusalem instead of for the syndicate's office for their support.

The trees look down and tell how they would act if you would be now the king that you used to be in the bright home where you hailed from. The zephyrs remember how you fanned your hair in the gardens of your native land. When you round the base of Olivet you begin to remember something you once knew, which broken hopes and faded heads cannot dull. And that is the day when it costs you nothing to live. You have no need of a set of tablets to record how many animals or men you have slain, or how many dollars you have invested, or how many sermons on sin you have preached, or how many people you have cured of sickness, or how many churches you have built.

In The Name of the Lord

It is not for these things the children sprang out of the factories, and the store, and the mines.

It was not for these things that the cities poured out their praises to Jesus of Nazareth, that carpenter's apprentice in the year of 30 of our count. No; it was because He knew His own name. He knew His own nature. Hear them chant: *"He cometh in the name of the Lord." "In the name of the Lord."* His works are not the refrain. They knew what he knew for that one supreme lesson to man. They knew that He knew the name.

And so it hath dropped down the centuries that He knew His Own Name and His Own Nature. But it has been hushed up that the Jerusalem spot in all men is the city point of their kingship. It has been hushed up that if one man knew his kingship and took it; if he also knew his ownership of all things and took it; if he also knew the secrets of nature and of man's nature, and the secrets of God the Mighty One; and knew himself to be the focus of the whole; and knew the Unspeakable Name, and knew that his own name would open like a two-leaved gate into all this knowledge, in His name would the Father send the Holy Ghost to teach all things and call all things to remembrance. But it is true. The children knew it for our sakes. The people knew it for our sakes. He made them know it that through the marches of the centuries His Name should have in it for all who would taste it the remembrance of their royal rights as kings with vested powers to let the light of Paradise on the world wherever they walked, and to hear the songs of the happy throng wherever they smiled, and to find the road of life a glad march.

There is one way of being provided for that has no flavor of hired labor in it, and that is what happens to all who face Jerusalem. There is one triumphal march of life for all of us, and that is the miracle that transpires for all who watch their own soul. There is one way of finding happy people everywhere, and that is by telling them the secret hosannas that will suddenly break out from the name Jesus Christ.

The Chicago Inter-Ocean Newspaper April 7, 1895

LESSON II

Easter Lesson
The Wicked Husbandmen

Mark 12:1-12

Today's religious treatment is like heat on invisible writing. It is certain to affect one's future dominating trait to read it. King Lear wanted fulsome flattery. Sincerity was less and less estimated by him. He had no knowledge of Mark 12. This chapter shows how some sly character trait is waiting in all men for the proper moment to flower into a great blossom of some sort. When Lear turned his daughter out of house and home because she would not overdose him with his favorite drug, he was really turning himself out of door.

We may have a most adroitly covered feeling that a former benefactor is better out of the way as far as we are concerned. We may even be geniuses at qualifying our praises of one to whom we are indebted for our present status, to the extent that people are subtly twisted out of favor with him. Some event or sentence will bring the whole of our secret feeling to light. Shakespeare makes one character declare: "The gods are just, and of our pleasant vices make instruments to scourge us."

This is a law of cause and consequence on the nether side — the side of our undermining mentality. Today's lesson uses this aide to illustrate our noble qualities with. There is one noble trait in you which the study of this lesson will bring out in all its glory.

The dark side of human nature is the favorite theme of writers, speakers, preachers.

The glorious side of his own history was the young carpenter's perpetual theme. He used just dark illustration enough to call the attention of his listeners and readers to his principles. They were familiar with the dark side, so they understood him better when he told them about dreadful things.

It is true that he understood himself so well that he could speak of himself as a rejected stone one moment and a constantly glorified body the next, and not be toppled to either object. He used himself for an object lesson for all mankind, and never got mixed up with what he said last. But was self-conscious every instant. As a general thing people get to being good and healthy by talking about goodness and health. They get to being thievish by talking about thieves. But this young peasant had struck his own base so that he was not good by talking on that side, nor bad by talking on that. He was what He was and talk could not reconstruct him. Meeting a multitude of people who were mixing themselves up in the two principles of good and evil by their tongues and minds, He told them a parable of one mighty fact in themselves, which they had ignored. It was the "I AM" of themselves, which could not be entangled with human life.

The Corner Stone of the Temple

Moses had known of its residing in him to some extent. David also had detected it. Each of the Buddhas had had an inkling. But it had been after all a covered up stone. Each man whom Jesus addressed thought of the Divine Absolute as a great mogul seated on a high dais beyond the stars, a very vengeful and unreliable character on some days and overindulgent on others.

"But, truly," said this great discoverer of his own greatness, "the Absolute is the uncontaminated One in yourself."

"He that receiveth you receiveth me, and he that receiveth me receiveth him that sent me."

This "I AM" in the Italian fruit vender is not identified with his putting the best berries on top. This "I AM" is not identified with the good policeman who arrests him. The good swings unobserved by the "Stone" "I am," and the bad flings its shades unpunished by that One.

15

Here was a man, Jesus, who was perpetually conscious of that uncontaminated "I AM." In looking at all sections and segments of his history let this fact not escape you. "In building for yourselves a world," said he, "you have ignored the one fact about yourselves which would cause you to wheel things perfectly."

He showed them that among the teachers of the day he represented the ignored "stone" of the "I am absolute authority." They would find it in their old books. Among the high statements of the prophets they would always find something about the "I AM" that is far above thoughts even when they are very splendid, and far different from conduct even when it is without flaw.

"My thoughts are not your thoughts, neither are my ways your ways."

The evil gifts you give yourselves by running your thoughts along evil statements are matched up by the good gifts you give yourselves by running your thoughts along good statements. Then again, good is always God over evil. It neutralizes a bad man's disposition to put his with a good one. Witness Joseph, who chemicalized eleven criminals within ten minutes after getting alone with them. Witness the sun worshippers who are self-radiant.

Destruction of Man's Self-Respect

It is sure destruction of a man's history to give up his mental vineyard to inferior subjects. He may have good books, good health, good religion, but if he occupies his mind with planning to get his name, his money, his constituency, by putting his "I Am" away out of sight and sound, he will find the plan a pell-mell business at some point. He will miserably destroy those husbandmen." "He" is the everlasting "I AM" hidden away out of memory in all people. History of human life is what this lesson sets plainly before us.

The manager of the mind is the chief husbandman who sits in the watchtower. (Verse 1) This is the human "I am." It is the chief of the affaire of life. It is lord of body. It makes mind brilliant or dull by its statements. It is the human mind that originates the propositions that God is one thing or another. It does not alter God to have ten million human "I am's" saying that he is in a dreadful state of mind because of the wretched lot of creatures he made out of dust once on a time. It only altereth the daily lot of those human "I am's."

Bear forever in mind that, however ignored, there is one "I Am" in all men which never created any Adams or Eves with tempers nor any serpents with deceptions. Jesus of Nazareth was acquainted with that "I Am." He here shows how the human manager of business life and health keeps no remembrance of that unidentified One. It is the "stone which the builders of human destiny reject." Often this Man, who took it upon himself to show the world what would happen to one man who did not forget his changeless and glorious Lord, called the differed "I am's" by the figurative word "stone."

Once he said: "God is able of these stones to raise up children" — of faith. Here he refers to the whole set of "I am's" — to the "I am happy," to the "I am ignorant," to the "I am all," to the "I am nothing." He shows how they may be raised up from saying such contradictory proclamations into a new light like unto the Shining One.

But today's lesson takes the talking and thinking human mind and shows it as forgetful of the awful majesty of the hidden "I AM." The lesson touches the instant when the wheel is come full circle.

The Human and the Absolute "I Am"

The human "I am" has not been paying any attention to the absolute "I AM," consequently all its riches are nothing when the wheel comes round. Its learnings are nothing when the wheel comes round.

That most beautiful, gracious, majestic, radiant teaching through time has been ignored. But as human wheels run down there shines the eternal "stone" which cannot run down. It is the unnamable comrade of all men. It is their ignored ever-present glory. It has a moment of appearing. It is the moment when the human governor, the changeable lord of the body who perches in his high estate as a mathematician, a musician, an artist, a preacher, a peanut seller, a typesetter, a school teacher, or some other performer in the garden of human life, has found out that the whole category is a set of movements needing another factor than either school or religion has brought forward.

On that day, when the human "I am" finds there is a teaching on this globe about the hidden "Lord," who seemeth to be so far away, that human "I am" will find its notions of all things "destroyed." (Verse 9)

And the hitherto rejected teaching will be the chief thing among men. (Verse 10)

This is the way the new race of people is to spring forth on this earth. The old teachings being all perished away, the old fashions will be gone. The old forms will be gone. The very people will be gone. Look abroad and gather up all that happened to this whole earth garden by reason of the human intellect rejecting the message sometimes arriving there, that there is no need of man's being limited to nature's dictates. How has that wise prophet "servant" been received by the husbandman?

Then how has this servant of man and of Deity been received? "Man is not a restricted being; he is a free, omnipotent spirit."

Then how has this highest of all proclamations been received? The only reality in man is his divinity.

Now Jesus Christ represented *in toto* these teachings. He stood there calmly as the moveless "I AM" that stopped at their center unseen, and told them so. At first they struggled. They opposed his representing their covered divinity and forcing its coverings to fall. But again it is a successful practitioner. They disappear as men and leave only their divine substance present.

On the face of these texts they appear to make out that on this occasion Jesus failed as a preacher of the divine in man, as the only reality of man.

But if he failed once he is not omnipotent. He makes his own proclamations null, "All power is given unto me in heaven and in earth."

Intellect, the Ruin of the Body

It was the same effect which Joseph had on the eleven criminals. They disappeared as criminals and appeared as noble lovers. They lifted up their voices and wept at first, but they became like Joseph next. So of these men whom Jesus addressed, they were roused to anger first, mixed with fear, and then Jesus Christ was left alone.

This lesson exhibits how a little attention to the "I AM" acts on the mind. It exhibits how no attention to it acts on the mind. It exhibits how absorbed attention acts.

Without any attention to the "I AM" in himself, an intellect will run its body to death, wear out its eyesight, close up its hearing and many other destructions, even when it sits in the highest tower of human power it can ascend. Witness the decrepit church dignitaries, school magnates, and kings and emperors, and queens and princes.

With a very little attention to it there is great uneasiness. There is perturbation. There is dissatisfaction. There is unrest. Witness the searching for new religious teachings, the antagonisms to old principles which describe God as a disappointed being. See how quickly those who have their eyes partly open detect a folly in your telling them that God wants men, large-hearted, noble men! They see at once that, as he made those men, he can have as many of them as he wants and of exactly the stamp he pleases.

Here is a sentence that with those who have attended their own untouchable "I AM," even a very little, will have no effect, except to turn them more decidedly to their marvelous fountain whence omnipotent power springs forth. "God has done all that infinite love can do to save us." It is a quotation from a celebrated Bible expositor. Looking straight around at the absolute "I AM" which is sometimes called God, we find that it does nothing. It moves not. The affect of looking at it is action, but it itself is moveless. The effect of looking at it is healing, but it is as devoid of health as the sun is devoid of boards. Looking at the sun, a tree grows tiers of boards. If the tree could talk it would have for one of its affirmations "My sun is board."

Fire and Invisible Handwriting
Looking at his majestic "I AM" a man sees that it grows through him and around him as entirely

new life from what he had while he was not looking at it.

At one stage he finds himself shrewder than he was before. At one stage he finds himself more lucky than he was before. At one stage he finds himself more generous. At one stage he is nobility itself. At a stage he is renewed. At one stage he feels the Jesus Christ power. At the final he is all Jesus Christ. The "I AM" has not changed, has not moved, but the watcher is a new man.

It sets like fire on invisible handwriting for a man to turn to the "I AM" that dwells in him, all his chaff is burned. All his nobility is exposed. Finally he is all gone except his self-consciousness.

This is what the lesson exposes. The self-conscious one was Jesus Christ. At one stage he was a man among men. At another stage he was the conscious recognition of self in all men. When religionists feel that consciousness of self, they call it finding Christ Jesus.

Inasmuch as Christ Jesus sometimes appears on this earth as self-conscious man, and again as interior recognition of power, they are right to call their quickened heart fire by his name.

The best kind of a god we can imagine is sure to let us take the consequences of our mistakes of ignorance. But the "I AM" burns away the ignorance and leaves intelligence. The "I AM" burns away all kinds of men except the Jesus Christ man and nobody is hurt by the fire. *"This was the*

Lord's doing and it was marvelous in our eyes."
(Verse 11)

Rejecting this pure fact will not alter its eternal excellence nor dim the day of its brightness on the earth.

Does not this lesson show forth plainly that there is a day for the full-orbed glory of the self-consciousness in all mankind to spring in sudden splendor from heart to heart as the lightning from the east unto the west? If the secret fault has its flowering time, and the noble trait has its blooming day, verily these shall swing aside like gates of gold, for the day of the sun of self-consciousness to shine — not consciousness of how to train thoughts and materiality, but consciousness of the hitherto ignored majestic "I AM."

The Chicago Inter-Ocean Newspaper April 14, 1895

LESSON III

Watchfulness

Mark 24:42-51

Man is an embodiment of the principle he accepts. If he is offered the principle that two plus two is four and stops at that regulation he finds that Sabbath point of "four" is his "Lord." If he accepts the Sabbath regulation that two has a certain purchasing power, that purchasing power is his "Lord."

It was the glorious province of Jesus Christ to proclaim: "The Son of Man is Lord of the Sabbath." It is no use to say that he meant the Jewish Saturday regulation only, because he took the two mites and by being Lord over their regulations compelled them to have more buying energy than all the Pullmans and Goulds in the temple. He was not exhibiting a province peculiar to himself, "All men are constituted this way," he said.

Today's text announces a fact. It is this: "Some day man finds himself tied up in the principle he has accepted." In other words: "*Ye know not what hour your Lord doth come.*" (Matthew 24:42) Some people have stated a proposition that hypnotic influence is an actual presence on this globe. They watch it. They maneuver with it. They have lectures on it. Suddenly they find it has come into them. They are an embodiment of it. They are hypnotic influences themselves. Their Lord whom they have sought has come. "The Lord whom ye seek shall suddenly come." One can be a seeker of a "Lord" by being afraid of it just as much as by loving it. We notice that Jesus here tells of a "lord" of whom the servant was afraid, but who came and sawed him open exactly as surely as he would have rewarded him with gold circles if he had loved him.

The main point is the "coming of the Lord." By this plain statement of the case of man we see well why it is that this chapter has been chosen by the committee on Bible texts for a quarterly temperance lesson. This committee points out in plain figures that by watching the intoxicating power of alcohol, praising it up for its energy and strength, rehearsing vigorously over and over how much greater it is than our combined manhood, etc., we have finally got that stuff to being an arrived "Lord." "It is even more a governor of man than bread," shouts a nicely printed, well reputed magazine. Not in these words exactly.

The Nether Workings of the Plenty System

It prints figures. They read: "Nine hundred millions of dollars for intoxicating liquors and five hundred millions for bread." Another set of men have "watched" the intoxicating property of alcohol till they have turned the principle of plenty wrong side up and are embodying the nether workings of the "plenty, plenty" system, of which man is spinningly capable, like a spider from his bosom. They have this system of plenty made up into some beautiful poetry which is very popular:

> *Plenty of poverty, plenty of pain,*
> *Plenty of sorrow plenty of shame,*
> *Plenty of broken hearts, hopes doomed and sealed,*
> *Plenty of graves in the potter's field.*

They say when there are a great many poor people in the United States is the day when the "Lord" of that poetry has arrived. Man is the originator of principles and systems. He spins them forth from his bosom as a spider spins her house. One day they have him fixed in their network.

It would have made a vast difference with the kind of "plenty" our citizens would embody if our young ones were taught from their cradles that the only "plenty," the only "Lord," they may expect is the prosperity of everywhere present loving kindness. It would make a vast difference to the intoxicating power of any preparation possibly concocted, if from the time they were born our people were told there was no intoxicating power in anything. Intoxicating power is a figment of spun imaginations which is lord or no lord, according to the principles we spin forth.

Nobody can dispute this, because Jesus taught it: *"They shall drink any deadly thing and it shall not hurt them."* This is when man stops reeling forth his principles and lets something at his headquarters exhibit itself.

We read this plainly in verse 44: *"In such an hour as ye think not the Son of Man cometh."* The "Lord" cometh while we are ceased from spinning forth principles to create as future "lords" over us. Then, when that which is truly "Lord" is plainly seen, how less than nothing is that sped forth "lord."

A great many principles are now ripening together. They were concocted at about the same dates of the spinning process and so are due about now. One is that an unscrupulous business man is sure to get the advantage of an honest one if the honest one does not watch him. So it is set down that the honest man must watch the rascal. This kind of watching is such a tax on the heads of men that they are all cracking and breaking up everywhere. It is now proclaimed that there is a great gloom settling down on the whole race in consequence of watching rascals. The "lord" whom men have watched has come. The rascal reigns.

Meaning of "Thine is the Power"

But Jesus Christ was not teaching us to watch a spun out fadge (bale of wool) originated by a few men in past ages. He was not speaking of being on the wakeful expectancy of disaster when he said, "Watch, therefore." Neither was he meaning that the intoxicating force which has been praised so much as so powerful was the one to be tacitly praying to when we are saying, *Thine is the kingdom and the power and the glory."* He would not teach me to declare an appetite was greater than myself. He would know that if I should pronounce an appetite to be a more powerful factor in my life than myself that every time I should be found saying, "Thine is the kingdom" I should really be talking to my appetite.

Whatever I proclaim as having me in its clutches is the god that seizes my praises when I am praying.

So business men are necessarily praying to turpitude when they are saying "Thine is the kingdom" if they have made the proclamation that corruption reigns. So religious people are necessarily talking to whatever they have announced as having the reins on this world when they say "Thine is the power."

In the sickroom the watcher keeps track of the disease. So it is proper that disease should flourish at about this date. And nurses and doctors may make certain that when they pray *"thy kingdom come, thy will be done,"* they will have more business than they can attend to, for they think that disease is a mighty power and health is a faint little plant with not much multiplying and replenishing energy in itself. So the disease principle seizes their prayers.

Under this dispensation it is reasonable to say that, *"the thing I feared is come upon me."* For poor Job, who found this out, had got twisted up in his Lord's clutches. His "lord" was a day of calamity. He had watched for that day for many years. It came.

But Jesus is here teaching me to stop watching those lords many and gods many instituted by my neighbors and prayed to by my clergymen, and watch for my rulership over my world. This lord in me shall make me ruler over rum, money, rascals, disease, death. Further than that, this lord in me maketh me ruler over life, health, prosperity, intelligence. And the springing into demonstration, visibility, governorship, of my lordship in myself, mine from before the world of phantasm, shall be very sudden. (Verse 50)

The Servant's Principle His Lord

In all these verses it reads outwardly as though it were the disposition of the Absolute One at the headquarters of man to punish him dreadfully for watching drunkenness, but it is the second rendering which shows that it is the servant's own principle that is his lord so terrible in vengeance.

"The Lord of that servant shall come in a day when he watcheth not for him." The man who believes in a punishment for not keeping his work up promptly is the slave, the servant of that principle.

30

The whole world has accepted and embodied that principle and it is a "lord" over mankind. Jesus Christ taught that he himself did all the work of the world once for all, and now there is nothing to do.

It is as much as the proclaimer in man can do to get free from the preaching of the sawing vengeance of that "lord" over this world and declare boldly that if the "working or starving" doctrine has such a world for its results I will take up with the offer of the Jesus Christ of this universe that my work and the world's work was done once and needs now none of our struggling.

This "servant" was at first under the principle of attention to daily labor. He got to watching another principle that men had taught him. This was at variance with the first one yet like unto it. He turned to watch the pleasures of drink which he had been warned against. The attention cannot turn two ways at once. When he had utterly forgotten the labor question it came to take possession of him. The doctrine that there is pleasure in intoxication is one with the doctrine that there is no damage in it. The results are the same. The fear of starvation operates the same as the love of starvation. Witness miser and vagrant. The fear of idleness operates the same as the love of idleness. Both kinds of people are unbearable. So both the hater and the lover are damaging to peace. The main point of the lesson is not that principles ripen but that they arrive when we least expect them, and that the Jesus Christ who is speaking says: "Watch me who have no punishment day, no prospering day, but am Lord over sin and goodness. As you watch me you will be me. You will see this suddenly, unexpectedly."

Labor Not For the Meat That Perisheth

The poor servant of principles and theories which other men have told him will soon find that not one of them has any sense in it. It is not necessarily so because Paul said it, that if any men will not work neither shall he eat. It is a principle, however, that now has thousands and tens of thousands by the neck, and they are very hungry simply because they have no work.

The glory of Jesus Christ is that his teaching was against working for your meat and bread, *"Labor not for the meat that perisheth."* The glory of Jesus Christ is that the moment any man honestly gives up thinking that he has to labor for his substance he will find that new position just as feeding as the other one. The Jesus Christ who is speaking through this section could tell how hatefully principles saw when they arrive, no matter how reasonable they have sounded when promulgated, but wanted it distinctly understood that he was not in the saws of any principle ever yet spun forth. He was "lord" over water and "lord" over wine. He was "lord" over their regular stopping places as drowners and intoxicators. He was "lord" over prompt, faithful, daily labor and its stopping place of death. He was "lord" over hypnotic suggestion and its stopping place of one human being's power over another. This was through self-knowledge.

"But the man who knows not himself," saith he, "is one moment under the regulation of working at some business, like a prince at his dressing or a car driver on the track, and the next moment under the regulation of the pleasure of or pain of alcohol. He may even get into the swinging saw of the spun-forth principle that a penny has the purchasing power which society has said. He may even get sawn and crunched in the full circle of the man-originated principle that it is evidence of goodness to be seeking after truth.

Let all men look unto me and they will suddenly see that they are not seekers after truth, but are all the shedders of truth. They will suddenly see that the works of the Jesus Christ man are truth, but that he is above the truth. "His 'lord' hath made him ruler." The sun is the heat of the world, but itself is more wonderful than heat. The sun is the color of all things, but itself is more wonderful than color. So Jesus Christ is the law of the heavens, but himself is more wonderful than laws. So Jesus Christ is a shedder of truth, but himself more wonderful than truth. This Jesus Christ, who so coolly shows how the world principles end up in a man, says plainly; "Whoever knows me sees me and ignores the world principles, and whoever sees me is myself. This being me is being thyself. And this being thyself out of the reach of the world is a sudden event, when thou art least aware."

The Chicago Inter-Ocean Newspaper April 21, 1895

LESSON IV

The Lord's Supper

Mark 14:12-26

In slipping hastily from our day of bondage to our day of freedom we leave some things undone, which we verily wanted to do. This is unleavened bread. The Jews ran away from Egypt where they were working night and day for a reward of kicks and thongs, and there was no time to leaven their bread.

Always in after times they had one day every year for commemoration of their Passover from Egypt to Canaan. Jesus kept this day with all the rest of them. "To the last of the earth," he said, "all men shall know that there is a way out of the gloomiest surveillance over your life by putting your hands on the moveless home of God under your feet and nigh your cheeks, and letting that mighty home find your home, and that awful Majesty defend you." There is a way of touching the splendor of eternity that makes it a fighter for you, and you do no contending. "I will contend with him that contendeth against thee." There is a way of putting up the eyes that lights them at the changeless vision of eternity, and now your eyes are shining and soul piercing and far-sighted to endless vistas.

Unleavened bread is the symbol of sudden freedom from misery. It stands for instantaneous demonstration. Let us eat the bread of quick health for this entire world. Let us drink the wine of quick inspiration for all this world. Let us kill the precious lamb of our pious talk about the long, long, days that it takes the Almighty to find us our free, happy home.

There is a way of putting out your hands on the home of the steadfast God and being so suddenly landed into your proper habitat that the lightning would blush at its loitering upon hearing that you had been ages on ages resting on the bosom of your mother in Canaan since it started in the east and struck in the west. For this touch of him that was from everlasting to everlasting discovers your oneness with eternity. It discovers to you what was and is and ever shall be.

The Meaning of Unleavened Bread

Today's lesson talks about finding our proper place in this world by killing the lamb of affliction and having left the unkillable fact of peace. "And the first day of unleavened bread, when they killed the Passover lamb, his disciples said unto him, *"Where wilt thou that we go and prepare the Pass-*

over?" And he replied: "A large upper room is fur-
nished and prepared."

"The first day of unleavened bread," is the first
instant we discover that we have something that
we walk on that is not ground, and something we
lean our heads on that is not chairs. "When they
killed the Passover lamb" is the first instant we
have stopped talking of time and change and loss
and danger. It kills delay and danger to stop talking them into bodies.

"His disciples said unto him," do the people
who want help; do they represent our own twelve
powers? "Where wilt thou that we go and prepare?" You will find that all is ready. It may seem
that we go somewhere that we find new friends,
that we are no longer seen in the streets of our
former city, but the other place had been long
waiting, the new friends had heard of us for years,
the home and the providing had been ready.

This is what leaning on the Almighty doeth.
"Put not your trust in princes." Even the crown
prince of Great Britain might fail you if you leaned
on his favor. Even your religion might cease to
console you in the day of your death. But, put out
your hand and touch the Eternal. Lean your face
on the Omnipotent. Long before the lightning has
generated itself in the alembic (something that
transforms or refines) of nature your two disciples
of touch and rest have found the pitcher of a new
life for you.

How to Escape From Sorrow

This lesson explains in a parable how easy and quick is the transit from sorrow to joy when the hands are stretched toward the moveless home of God, so nigh the newsboy and the czar and me. It allows how sudden is the transit from death to bounty when the face has once felt the upbearing God of whom men have talked, but whose splendors they reserve for by-and-by.

It is truly better to taste and see and touch this Almighty Presence than to talk about it. And this is eating the lamb. What is talked is so certain to touch the bitter herb of delay, but what we touch and taste and lean upon is what was long ago prepared for us.

This lesson shows that all the people of this world want something different from the way it is now going on with them externally. It gives the secret of quick transit from the present hatefulness that glares and growls, that has come from talk, to the majestic uplands of happiness that lie so still under their feet and that do not come from talk but from touch.

There is a mansion under the feet and close to the head of the most famine-stricken son of talk.

There is a way to ignore what is said about what we ought to do and what we ought not to do and find what is already done. Let the meanest of us kneel down on the swelling hill of eternity that resteth under our feet and it hath the mystery of providence for us. Then while we are sleeping the stones and the stars of nature, the hands and the tongues of nations, are conspiring to protect and befriend and provide for us, and they cannot help themselves. The energy of this that my feet stand upon, the speed of this that my hands do touch, passeth speech.

The Lord Shall Defend and Deliver

Run, flee from your hard place, your dark place, your unrequited place, to the glory under your feet. And *"as the birds flying so will the Lord defend thee, and defending also he shall deliver. For the Lord of hosts will fight for Zion."* This is more wonderful than truth. It is what was before the truth word dropped its assurances on our heads. Never mind the truth. Mind the mountain top of the eternal home under your feet and close by your head. It is truth that the minister tells when he says that flesh is grass, and the days of man are a shadow; it is truth he tells when he says that errors make sickness and death. But study no truth. Lean on the substance that was in the place it now is before ever the stars strung their golden beads on the necks of the millions of millions of midnights before primeval man wept for the loss of his home.

This parable of the Lord's supper in the prepared guest chamber must not stop at the tiresome talk of a Judas and a coming crucifixion. It must baptize the heights of inspiration with the same enchanting waters of meaning that it does the mind that reads only of the prescient vigor of a martyr in the verses.

At the heights of inspiration we find that the responsibility of finding our places and duties is not resting upon us. By the irresistible turns of this Almighty One we are suddenly at the table of comradeship, with power and wisdom and illumination. We know what to do and it is easy. We know what relation we bear to this world of men and women.

The intellect says that the child is deformed because the senses say so. Whoever lets go of his intellect finds that the child is not deformed. It is not till intellect yields itself up as nothing that the divine intelligence is plain. As they sat at meat Jesus told them that Judas would betray him to illustrate how the intellect judges. He would soon say that the divine in man was a latent and unreliable power, not nearly as secure a protection as money, not nearly so safe as business partnerships. {Is this really what she is saying? That the 'divine' in man is unreliable – is she using 'divine' as NOT divine the way we think of it? Does she mean 'intellect' here as 'divine'?}

Whenever a man says, "Trust in God and keep your powder dry," he is a Judas. Jesus did not keep powder dry and did not so teach men. He told them that the Almighty "I AM" was sufficient. Even Moses was wiser in the "I AM doctrine than to arm up the Jews with sling stones when they had the army of Egypt after them. There is no defense like the "I AM." Touch it as it spreads its omnipotent arms under your feet. Lean against it as it rises higher than the hills by your side. "You are safer to have a million dollars in your pocket," says the businessman either by adroit turns or straight speech. Even this silent idea is Judas. And every trait of character we possess is sorrowful or downcast when the intellect is about to be self-hanged. For John and Peter and Simon and Matthew, and the whole tribe, have had great respect for intellect. (Verse 19)

<u>Intellect Is the Great Guide</u>

John stands for our stingy nature, our carefulness of our hard-earned earnings or our patrimony. Intellect has explained to our careful provisions for ourselves and family that that is an excellent trait. Intellect points out the downfall of spendthrifts. The intellect always leaves out, however, that there is no limit to the possessions of a man who has his hands on the Omnipotent One, whose feet walk on the Almighty. Poor John! He amounts to nothing but a scared baby till Judas is gone — quite gone. Then John blooms out as a free grace, unstinted power, unlimited riches, as lavish as nature.

There is Peter, also. We all have the Peter trait, but it amounts to nothing but conceitedness, pig-headed blundering, till Judas is gone — quite gone.

Then the Peter trait of wanting to have our own way everywhere we go blooms out as instantaneous inspirational healing power.

There is also our Simon trait of self-pity and pity of our neighbors. This trait is pandered to by the intellect of the nineteenth century so much that we really pity the heathen, we pity the tea-drinkers, we pity the newsgirls. But we never would have any pity if the intellect did not insist upon it that God made such hard lines and bad inheritances for some people and gave such good opportunities to others.

When the intellect is gone — quite gone — by its own choice, up springs that pitying trait into a sudden power to hurl aside the miseries and misfortunes caused by talks and thoughts of intellect

Such is the effect of a man watching with all his faculties toward the Jesus Christ in himself that he begins to quake because all the faculties realize somewhat that they are not absolute to the Jesus Christ, but are training still under intellect.

It is the reasoning voice of the Jesus Christ spirit that says: "Though Judas deceives concerning my providing and protecting power, it will not be for long. He will soon perish. Good were it if intellect had not been managing things, but I drink the wine of God to be your only inspiration."

Twelve Traits of Character
This seems a difficult matter to make positive to men. But the fact remains that the twelve pow-

ers or traits in each man are feeble and puerile till the intellect is self-surrendered and the inspirations of spirit have wined and enlivened them. This doctrine is the blood of the new covenant, which is shed for all. (Verse 24)

The fact remains that Jesus of Nazareth took twelve men, each representing a trait in each of us, and caused the intellect to destroy itself under the name Judas and rise up again as inspiration. After this event all the men who represented our traits of character became most wonderful and powerful beings. The fact remains that this doctrine is certain to be the wine and blood and strength of a new type of men when it is received. The fact remains that we sing a new song as we feel the omnipotent presence of the Everlasting One, and we go as new beings into our mountains of majesty. We no longer walk the earth; we walk on God, the moveless home of the soul. We no longer lean on the chairs and the business undertakings, or the ways that we were wont, for our support, our information, our friends, our rights. We lean on the eternal substance that is the changeless friend of the soul. It is nigh, very nigh to our faces; it is nigh, very nigh, to our hands. And feet born of stepping on it overcome the world. And hands born of touching it are masters of destiny. "For whatsoever is born of God overcometh the world."

Let us sing this wonderful hymn, for Judas is now to cease forever. Intellect is bursting itself all over the globe that the inspirations of the Christ Jesus man may ennoble and waken our faculties from first to last.

The mighty ones of heaven arise among the nations when Judas has performed his last act of buying man from looking to the Almighty to lead and defend and provide. The quickness of the Omnipotent is in its having been always what it is as home and light and safety for all.

The Chicago Inter-Ocean Newspaper April 28, 1895

LESSON V

Jesus In Gethsemane

Mark 15:42-52

Cowper attributed to the direct interposition of Divine Providence his driver's inability to find the right spot in the river where he had planned to drown himself. This made him write; "God moves in a mysterious way."

It is possible for us all to get such a taste and touch of the protecting and defending forces occupying the spaces, that accidents and misfortunes fall aside from us. No matter what we should do or say, or what or who should be pitted against us, we should always be safe and free. United with security itself there is no danger anywhere.

The divine security to which Cowper had somewhat allied himself was the Father unto which Jesus of Nazareth was entirely committed. At every instant of his career he was safe, free, untrammeled Spirit. Knowing this he found himself surrounded by a world of mankind denying the right to absolute security for themselves. He found them believing in the excellence of death and suffering. It was their strongest mental conviction. They carried it into every movement. Unless somebody or something could be hurt by their speech or conduct they had no pleasure in it.

So great was this belief in mankind that they felt that the absolute and changeless God was perpetually employed in tormenting people.

The crowning act of the man Jesus was his concentration of all this world belief into his Own Mind and in that alembic neutralizing it and chemicalizing it by His Own security from danger till all the world might by acquaintance with him go secure forever from danger and pain without the charge of cowardice being laid to them.

It was the boldest action of mind ever undertaken by any man, and in his boldness all men who touch His Spirit are bold, not through ability to challenge that deity who loveth to torment, but through being secure from torture like as is the Free Spirit. The boldness of the Spirit, whether we call it Holy Spirit or Divine Spirit, is its non-expectancy of being hurt. The everywhere-spreading splendor of the divine Presence is its non-expectancy of being tortured. Therefore if a man expects afflictions from the hands of his God he expects what the hands of God do not hold to give him, and is simply assuming premises and arguments about the Absolute to suit himself.

These Are Strangers to Jesus

"Why have ye made the heart of the righteous sad whom I have not made sad, saith the Lord?" Is it affirmed by anybody that Jesus of Nazareth was not acquainted with that Lord who never made anybody sad? Had he not wrested with that Lord till he was exactly like Him? Then he suddenly struck the moment when all the dread of pain and the shrinking from anguish common to sentient creation was neutralized in Himself. He felt the name, the character, the splendor of the Secure One. As bone of bone, flesh of His flesh, mind of His mind. From that day acquaintance with Jesus Christ should be for all men entire security from anguish of mind. *"My peace give I unto you."*

If anybody now imagines he has coming ordeals he certainly is not thoroughly acquainted with Jesus Christ. If anybody expects he must rouse himself to face the future with a brave front he certainly is not acquainted with Jesus Christ. *"For your joy no man taketh away."* And, *"God is Spirit." "Be ye as God." "I am God."* These are the reasonings that spring from messages to man.

By knowing that one man has taken the whole force of the entire world's error or sin with respect to the tormenting employments of Jehovah we perceive that we do not need to carry any moiety (two equal parts) of such belief. We need expect no pain or misfortune. Such expectation is pure assumption on our part. Jesus Christ took that mental state once for the race. We need anticipate

47

nothing, "By His self-elected stripes we are healed."

It is not the greatness of ability to bear mental dread that comes with acceptance of Jesus Christ's well-done task, but the greatness and enchantment of a security as free and careless as that of the untouchable smiling spirit itself.

The Holy Ghost Never In Terror

It is not probable that the Holy Ghost was ever in terror for dread of being sewn asunder or punished for an accident. Jesus of Nazareth was as fearless and safe in mind and body as the Holy Ghost that spreadeth its white beauty through the stellar spaces. But He loved the world. Bold as the lion of the tribe of Judah was the love of Jesus for the world. "Come, anguish of mother heart, anguish of martyr and galley slave, come! Come, fear of chastisement in child of the tyrant and serf of the manor house, come! Come, fear of the wrath of a vindictive Jehovah, filling the breast of preacher and saint. Come! I will deny you your right on this earth."

The mother can spring with strength born of one sight of the secure Spirit from crag to crag of unscalable mountains in protecting her baby free from threatened hurt, but He of Calvary, through all sight of security, sprang from crag to crag of unscalable Gethsemane for you and me. We need not dread the lash of tongues or the thongs of fate. Safe as the child sleeps while the mother defends it, as we may rest on the secure bosom of a great fact in the universe, namely, that all anguish of mind was once borne well and wisely, once for all men, and from that day all mental anguish is self-imposed, but not called for, not necessary, and supreme evidence of not understanding Jesus of Nazareth.

That which is least burdened is lightest. That which knows how to evade burdens best is securest. He who has no burdens through annulling burdens is free security in himself.

"There shall be a handful of corn on the top of the mountain, the fruit whereof shall shake like Lebanon. And His name shall endure forever."

Last Act of the Heaven-Inspired Senses

The spirit of Jesus of Nazareth is the unburdened Spirit of this planet. So unburdened that the highest mountain top is not higher than its unweighted lightness ascends. But acquaintance with that lightness is the assurance of all men that they need charge no more their minds with dread of being hurt, or fear of loneliness. It is the last act of the heaven-inspired Jesus in his self-treatment undertaken for the sake of a race, that he concentrates the desertion of friends at the hour when most needed, the indifference of friends at the instant when the heart begs hardest, and finds himself free from friends forever, not through inability to charm and interest them, but, in the chemical laboratory of his own mind, detaching himself from the weight of friendship and sympathy that in his supreme freedom I might be supremely free.

As in thy light I see light, so in thy freedom I am free. The fruit of that free day called Gethsemane shall be the absolute freedom from mental bondage for all this world.

It is a mental thralldom to be clinging to human beings for confirmation of our office and for sympathy in your undertakings. Jesus clung once, and let go once, and became the free handful of corn on the mountain top of supreme isolation once, and since that time acquaintance with Jesus Christ has meant, and forever will mean, self-supporting, self-inspiring, self-honoring spirit for high, low, rich, poor, bond, free, Jew, Greek, male, female, world without end.

The Glorious Army of Martyrs

There had been martyrs before Him, good, noble, divinely faithful. Like the mother who saves the baby by one glance toward the secured God, so they gave man the way of honor through sight of brave endurance of torture. They caught one glance of the worthiness of honor in the true God, and that sight called for their highest gift, which in all ages has been suffering.

If man could only suffer enough they felt they would honor God enough. But on the heights of supernal wisdom it is understood that sight of the secure God covers all other sights.

Worthy is the Mighty One, inhabiting eternity to receive honor and glory and praise and offerings. Sight of that worthiness has inspired the self-oblation of sage and saint, man and child and maiden. Wonderful is the wisdom of the majestic God; sight of that wisdom has tipped the pens of warriors with transfixing flames. Tongues have roused armies and nations when moved by minds catching sight of the wisdom splendor of the everlasting Father, but sight of the Secure One was the sight of Jesus Christ. Secure goes man forever from the clamp and clinch of suffering when he sees the secure God. Secure goes man forever free from the crowd and bind of ignorance when he sees the secure Supreme.

Jesus of Nazareth saw the secure Supreme and saw the frightened mind of man all in Himself. Contending and alone He seized upon security from dread of hurt and love of human comradeship, and saw in the chemistry of God how free all men might be. One step further in the bold one's alchemy. He would expose the free God to all who would accept his sight of security as their sight, and thus be not only security itself, but instantaneous unburdening for all the world without their struggle to press past the evils of suffering and ignorance hung up by the dogmas of suffering preached by imaginations.

"He that hath seen Me hath seen the Father."

End of the Dreary Day

Struggle to find the mighty Father whom to find is happy freedom forever, was once mad, once for all this world. We do not need now to struggle to find the free state of the Absolute. This Man has offered us the sight of eternal, unweighted, smiling security. Through the acknowledgment of His offer the mystery is wrought. The long, hard days are ended. The journey is closed. And we did nothing to shorten the days, and nothing to lighten the burden except to accept the tremendous offer of Jesus Christ as the healer of hardships, the healer of all clinging friendships, the healer of all fear of hurt, and of struggle to find the right God. He found the security of heaven once for me and by my accepting the offered security the miracle of my quick transit from darkness to light is wrought; the miracle of my instantaneous journey from pain and prison to peace and wide range takes sudden place.

Jesus was not only a martyr; he was martyred that I might not be a martyr. Accepting His healing office I am lifted out of martyrdom; even the martyrdom of environments, on the wings of miracle after miracle wrought by the enchantment of Gethsemane's masterly Victim and victory everywhere now present on this earth. (Mark 14:32-42)

The Chicago Inter Ocean Newspaper May 5, 1895

LESSON VI

The Jesus Christ Power

Mark 14:53-72

There is one central Judgment in all mankind. Today's international golden text proclaims that it "is despised and rejected" of men. This central judgment has twelve signs of power. Sometimes the signs of power appear to be signs of feebleness. Did not Peter whose quality represents instantaneous formulation of words act like a coward and a simpleton? Yet these performances were turned into strokes by which the shining judgment within himself called attention to itself.

In a dumb, silly, blind way, men nowadays sometimes proclaim that they are also Jesus Christ. They show no signs of the Jesus Christ Powers. They show none of the Jesus Christ character, but their apparently silly proclamation is the first strike out of one of those twelve powers that are folded around their central judgment.

They are not despising and rejecting their interior divinity, but they command no respect by their infantile manner of announcing it. Peter wanted to coerce the soldiers into believing in Jesus Christ, so he cut off the ear of poor Malchus. But the glory of the central judgment is its peaceableness and kindness. Instantly his blunder was transmuted into a practical demonstration of the healing tenderness of the central judgment. As an intellect he was a blunderbuss; as a judgment he was a healing miracle.

This occurred when the Jesus Christ of him put out his hand and healed the ear. It had once been promised Peter that no mistake he ever made should count against him and every good word he spoke should work like magic. *"Whatsoever thou shalt bind on earth shall be bound in heaven, and whatsoever thou shalt loose on earth shall be loosed in heaven."*

It is well known in metaphysics that binding is formulation by affirmation, and loosing is unformulating by denials. As if I say that I am unhappy, when I am not especially so, I may count upon it that my words will formulate into a state of unhappiness for me by and by which will perhaps be almost unbearable.

The Negative Side of Peterism
Some people write letters detailing their miseries, and mourn to their neighbors about their misfortunes, when if you examine into their affairs they are not bad at all. But their words are fixing

up futures for them, and in due season all that they lament over will arrive. This is Peterism on the negative side, but the central judgment melts their words, and they will know enough to write long letters describing their happy fortunes, their pleasant surroundings. They will put out these affirmations for the sake of a future crop.

Jesus taught this lesson once under the figure of a man building a house and sitting down beforehand to count the cost. What will it cost me in the matter of a future set of conditions to declare now that I am wretchedly unhappy? It is not a question of how I now feel, it is a question of my next year's house.

I built this present set of affairs by affirmations last year or ten years ago or the more (there is a sentence missing here) sure he will feel that he has more than a model of the whole glory thereof shall suddenly break forth through all his twelve gates.

This omnipresent man within man is denied by the word of man. It is tried, convicted, slain the instant we say that we have not felt it, do not know it, and that it is sacrilege to affirm its existence in all men.

Old System is a Dead Failure

The high priest is that Simon trait in us that wants the world to think and act our way, right or wrong. It listens to no absolute fact because it was not brought up that way. We love the present systems with that Simon trait and it is almost

impossible to get it to see that the old systems are
a dead fight. But civilization which has ripened
says the old system is a failure, and the only good
visible was wrought by somebody getting his
Simon trait melted away by turning to look at the
central judgment in himself long enough to strike
up a new statement.

Martin Luther looked long enough to get a
statement that it melted a system or two which
were pushing like a high priest of Mark was. *"And
with the high priest were assimilated, all the chief
priests and the elders and the scribes."* It is a section meant to show how religious men, scientific
men, learned Masoners and financial schemers
refuse to acknowledge the possibility of the common divinity. They listen to the good old dogmas
about how ignorant and wicked men are. They do
not pay heed to the new statement, not material of
we want, (something is not quite right here .. ?)
then it is to show forth illuminations of strength-
ened wisdom.

This whole section represents the twelve powers of man determined not to yield to their new
judgment when it begins to rise. Is it not common
given now for us all to expect more of the present
systems than of the new on what we see is arising?

What is more certain than that the money
power in the present society, and state is to be
demolished with the heat of the spiritual science
now rising in the East? Yet who stands up and lets
go of his money in supreme conscience that he

shall want for nothing if he lets it go? If he should do this he would be Simon transmuted. The spiritual science now spreading its fine, subtle radiance through the subconscious mind of anyone is entirely capable of defending and supporting its believers. They will soon be providing this on new lines. But even if they stayed afar off from actual test of its powers (not a complete sentence). (Verse 54)

Conflicting Testimony on the Spirit Power

There is conflicting testimony on the subject of the actual power of the spirit in man. "It teaches us to speak the word and get good jobs at sawing wood or at syndicating nature's gifts," say some high priests. It teaches us that while we are in the world we must do as the world does, says the mind of man who makes high statements concerning the spirit, but he sees how powerful is the artificial standard men are given to. (Verse 54) That is, Peter afar off winning himself with the servants of present methods. Keeping on the side of the capitalists and governors.

The Omnipresent presence is here, however, here in its arrived radiance. The kings tremble and the presidents hug their bags of gold thinking it must be that as the things that have been heretofore powerful, they are powerful. But it is not gold, that high seats of honor, not intellectual power that can avail us as we stand now at the bar of the downfall of nations. It is only the spiritual quality that can give with safety in its wings. *"I am, and ye shall see."* (Verse 62)

It is possible for man to be saved from swords, serpents, fires, and guillotines, by the rise of this spiritual judgment teaching him new ways of safety, and new lines of happiness. This lesson teaches that it (whole sentence missing here) affirmations are guiding, just practice for one year with negative affirming, that you are already a bankrupt. See if the forces of the Universe do not conspire, hustle, rustle, draw, drive all things to bankrupt you.

Use affirmations on the negative or miserable side and the Peter before taking the spiritual medicine and use affirmations on the positive or joyous side and be Peter after taking spiritual medicine. The Jesus Christ announcement acts like medicine on affairs and minds. The lesson of today is taken from Mark's account of Jesus Christ and the negation of Jesus Christ. Mark shows mankind just having heard of their own central divinity and not daring to bend to it because it is not a fighting character. Probably there is nothing that smartens a man like seeing how little fight there is in the omnipotent spirit that he sees in Jesus Christ.

"The non-resisting, non-fighting central judgment knows that it owns the universe and there is nobody in that universe but itself; it is often majestic to fight shadows so it keeps still. *"He held his peace."* (Mark 14:61)

No Substance in Error
Let it here be known that all talk about fighting error is Peter cutting off ears. All knowing Jesus Christ shows there is no substance in shadows and that is healing ears. Today we fight liquor, we fight bribery, we fight to barter. With what results? Do they increase or decrease? Just so, if the Jesus Christ of the fighting Peter had not come forth, should the soldiers have pounced upon Peter himself and we would have had no victory of his entrancing miracles.

Mark knows how this affirmation and denial power is to us, is transmuted by the Jesus Christ judgment. Many people are disputing that there was an actual man Jesus Christ and that if there were not, and the history of this was only a fabrication of the four men — Matthew, Mark, Luke, John? Is there not a possibility of such greatness in providing the uncovering of the Omnipotent Divinely concealed in his heart's center?

We are told that the twelve disciples of Krishna, Buddha, and Christ are the storyteller's art of personifying the twelve constellations or signs of the zodiac, which were known to remote antiquity. Christ represents the sun which rises in the sign Virgo (born of a virgin), and during the summer solstice passing everyday higher until it crosses the meridian. Here we get the story of the judgment. Then as the sun descends, bringing summer to another hemisphere, we have the story of the descent into hades. Now as thou wilt not suffer thy holy one to reside in hell so we have the home-coming and again under the story of resurrection from the dead.

We have the story of King Arthur and his twelve knights of the round table to illustrate the sun and the twelve signs. We have the story of Charlemagne with his twelve paladins. Any cyclopedia will give a summary. We have Jacob and his twelve men. We have our inner judgment and its twelve powers which are weak and bombastic when the judgment sun shinning somewhere reigns, but all glorious when our judgments are shining toward them.

Dangers of Historic Revelation

History always as it gets further back, gets less believable; so Jesus as a historic character gets less and less convincible unless you feel the stirring fire of your own divinity, and feel the good of a power at work with your words and actions that is not ordinary. Do great men feel certain that it was their own worthiness and wise efforts that won them their victories? When a composer has tried, tried, and tried and terribly tried to write what the world would praise him for, did he get the praise? No, when there was his next door neighbor who carelessly composed some arrangement of tones and semi-tones, and the world got down and kissed the hem of his garment at the sound of the ravishing bow. Does he feel that the earned that praise? No.

"Not unto him the honor" is the honest acknowledgment of greatness. Unto what, then of
the honor? I will tell you. It is to the naming glory
of that inner sun that rests at the center of all
alike. The story of Jesus Christ makes it possible
for all men everywhere to know how to have (sentence missing here) judgment. "It ought to be
hushed up, and all those proclaiming it ought to be
imprisoned," is often said in these very days.

"They ought to stop at regarding sickness as
intellectual delusion, and let sin alone," say the
great high priests of modern theology. But the
spiritual in man throws the new light on wicked-
ness and finds it is as much an intellectual
delusion as disease.

The spiritual judgment in man throws the
mysterious light of a new dispensation over sorrow, and there in the Orient, where in the sorrow
is the crowning conqueror, shows that the focal-
ized exponent of the world sadness, the Dali Lama,
is the victim of the intellectual delusion.

No Resurrection for Sin and Sorrow
Evil is delusion. Matter is delusion. Sorrow is
delusion. Sickness is delusion. Death is delusion.
The Sanhedrin sat in a semi-circle at 2 o'clock in
the morning, hugging delusions.

But the night was broken, the morning was
dawning. The spiritual man was there prophesy-
ing this day. What happened in Jerusalem the
ancient, now happens on a whole globe. Jesus
himself said that when his name had been told to

all countries his judgment would strike all hearts. And this is the glory of the dawn upon us of what was prefigured that night in Jerusalem, namely, that it is not the spirit which is to be buried out of sight, and covered with stones this time; it is all that which judgeth against the spirit.

The wheel has its other side and that is uppermost now. The Sanhedrin had half the circle and their say for lo! these 1900 years; but Jesus had the other half of that circle and it is his turn now. It is not Jesus who goes under the sod at this descent, but the Sanhedrin of whatever opposeth the Spirit.

Sin goes under now never to rise again. Sorrow goes under now, and for it there is no resurrection. Barter and deal, injustice, poverty, oppression, falsity, go down now with the subtle radiance of this spiritual light that is arising in millions of hearts.

He cometh on the right hand of power. (Verse 62) That is the healing, uplifting, inspiring, positive way of speaking which the spiritual quality uses. The opponents rent their clothes in that moment to prophesy; how rent should be the systems that have hidden the spirit in man when its reign should begin in this age. (Verse 63)

The signals of rending are at our doors, the rending is at their heels. But fear nothing. Though the death, the burial, the darkness, the violence, were assigned to the Jesus Christ man, they are discovered to belong only to the opposite traits:

and the opposite traits are all intellectual, ethical delusions. It cannot hurt a delusion to die. So it is promised that this new dispensation shall enter softly.

The Chicago Inter Ocean Newspaper May 12, 1895

LESSON VII

Jesus Before Pilate

Mark 15:1-15

Sitting at his table, a chemist learns to tell whether a drop of water came from the Amazon River or the Atlantic Ocean, though he never saw either.

Periclea was never seen except on one street in Athens, namely, the one leading from the Senate Chamber to his lodgings, and that was the key to his mastery of the art of legislation. Socrates charged one of his students a double fee because he had to teach him how to keep still and draw his forces home to himself.

Mirhanoya is the withdrawal of diffused being to a fine, independent point. This is undivided, unscattered intelligence. It has been the province of modern metaphysics to hammer perpetually on the main propositions of Schopenhauer and Berkeley. It makes no difference to the facts of a case whether I believe in them or not. It makes some difference in my skill in managing my affairs if I dispute facts, but the facts abide in unchanged security indifferent to my disputes.

Today's Bible lesson is an illustration of the personal practice of Mirhanoya or the withdrawal of man's whole mind to himself and standing in undivided self-consciousness. As Jesus stands there with the majestic silence of one who does not even project an idea forward for an expert mind reader to get hold of, he knows that he could convert Pilate into a servile slave or an unreliable king by one willful movement of his moveless mind. He knows with masterly intelligence what metaphysicians are hammering perpetually upon but have never practiced to extremity; that is, he knows that the external, material, moving world is my mental presentation. He knows it is his mental presentation. He declines to present any more such men as he has been presenting, or any more such scenes as he has been painting by thinking. He declines to think.

The Golden Text Wisely Chosen
He has drawn himself to himself that he may see that world and that being which were uncreate. He stands at Mirhanoya, the sand grain point of undivided self knowledge. He thinks nothing. He speaks nothing. He stirs not. *Ecce homo* (behold the man) (Mark 15:1-16)

Therefore the golden text is wisely chosen: *"Jesus yet answered nothing, so that Pilate marveled."* If anybody does not believe that he sees a world exactly like his thoughts let him change his thoughts and discover what a different world he will find.

The suspicious man will find flaws in Jesus. The ambitious man will find a rival in Jesus. The suspicious man will turn every movement into an artful plan to do harm. The ambitious man will regard every praise of him as his sly encroachment on his rights. *Ecce homo.*

At the Pilate scene enacted by Jesus of Nazareth he is taking intrinsic man as he walks this planet and, in full understanding of him, makes a full exhibition of what kind of projected opinions of him cover him. Some see murderous natures everywhere, and they finally build crosses, guillotines, gallows to destroy them on. But they do not destroy murderers by this process, for they keep right on projecting ideas that keep covering intrinsic man with signs of guilt.

The withdrawal of thoughts home to himself to think no more made Jesus the most silent man of history. So silent was he this day before Pilate and the elders that he was pure God. Knowing his thinking equipments he would not use them. He can see Pilate's intrinsic nature covered by the opinions of men. He can see the shining Jesus in every elder who faces him. He sees himself in them and sees only himself unshaded by ideas. They see their own ideas in him as the mother sees her opinions of her child when she punishes him and not the child itself.

Watchman, What of the Night?

How runs it with the world with its eyes on its ideas and not on the great fact of the case?

What of the night, oh, watchman? Do crimes increase as thou chasest the criminal in the ever present Jesus who stands up in all men? Do beggars and mourners multiply as thou chasest them up, hanging thy ragged notions on the kingly Jesus that standest owning not only earth but heaven in the tramps and disheartened?

The world is my own mental presentation. It represents my ideas. But Jesus taught me to stop having ideas, to stop receiving ideas; he taught me to be. This, he assures me, stands me up in my own place, discovers unto me my original kingship, and makes me satisfied with myself, independent of jeers and condemnations, an unkillable, unspoilable me, hurting nobody, and misrepresenting nobody; understanding all things and all people through first understanding myself.

"The spiritual man judgeth of all things, but is himself judged of no man."

The Pilate hunter sees Pilates in Jesus. To reign in undisturbed autocracy is the Pilate idea. "The religious people, the merchantmen, the laboring men, let them keep quiet while I govern to suit myself. Can you do that?" he asks the Jesus man. "I can," is the simple answer. He does not explain that the splendor of governing is not governing.

Whose reign is softly glowing now over the hills of time, his who never used his governing thoughts and will by moving men and things to agree with his ideas, or Pilate's whose career was our modern system of exercising thought and will to the utmost to conquer destiny and neighbors?

Silence the Secret of Power

What made Napoleon great? Because he knew how to keep his thoughts so still that nobody could read his mind. If any man knows how to keep his ideas so still that nobody can catch them from him he will know all about his neighbors, their character, motives, and habits by the questions they ask of him and by the accusations they make against him. They can get no cue from him, and so they show their own hands *nolens volens* (unwilling or willing).

"The chief priests accused him of many things, but he answered them nothing." Ho! Ye who accuse, know ye not that the one ye are accusing is so silent that as in a pool ye are in him witnessing your own manner of mind?

Behold how many things they witness against the Jesus in their midst. (Verses 3, 4, 5) To the proud he is proud. To the sensual he is sensual. To the autocrat he is a usurper. To whom is the Jesus even now in our day, ever the Jesus indeed? Had they not the laws of the land, the religion of the people, the social customs of A. D. 30 to sustain their opinions? Have we not our pulpit preachers, our city mayors, our judges and juries, our detectives and policeman, our missionaries and social purity battalions to testify that Jesus is a criminal when they look at him in the masses? But, though I see the criminal in you, the hypocrite in you, the liar in you, the eternal fact will remain that you are Jesus.

Judgment of the World Powerless

Hush the clatter of your grieved thoughts, your angry thoughts, caught from accusing minds, and, standing at Mirhanoya, still self knowledge, witness how powerless the judgments of a world can be. And you will thus be practicing Jesus in the Pilate hall.

Be so moveless that nobody can read your thoughts. You will be practicing Jesus in the Pilate hall. Be so still that no thought stirs on the crystal sea of being and you will be practicing Jesus getting ready to rule from pole to pole, King of kings, and Lord of lords.

The multitudes let Barabbas loose on the world at the suggestion of the chief envy man. (Verse 10) "Who shall stand before envy?" cried Solomon. When the envy sees Jesus he sees a rival. Do you see a possible rival at every turn? Do you see competition everywhere? What is Jesus you are competing with? That is Jesus you see as a man competing with and against his fellow man.

Ideas Which Have Grown Wearisome

But what is Jesus doing? Nothing. Why does he nothing? That he may do all. What think you of

Jesus? Though you should run your diction to such splendid syllables that congregations would fall down in weeping adoration, you have nowhere touched the golden glory of the still king, whose beautiful presence is here in our midst accused of being a felon one day and a millionaire the next. You are only seeing your ideas, and people are tired of your ideas. They want the still Jesus who waits here to reign. Good ideas and bad ideas have run their wearisome circuits, fetching the same round of good men and bad men into view age on ages and no satisfactory times yet out of such squirming turns of minds, fashioning men after their own imaginations. And there never can be. Cease from thoughts. Be so silent that all the people tell thee their secrets, but thine are buried in thine intrinsic kingship of silence. This is practicing Jesus.

When did the Nazarene say that his reign should flash from East to West? Was it not when he and his God should be named as one?

"In that day ye shall ask the father in my name."

The Pain and Shame of False Witness

Climb upon the hilltops of fearless peace and there you will find that though Jesus Christ was scourged and crucified outwardly once, letting the small temple area in Jerusalem show by its vivid object lesson how it is forever the Jesus in man that is bruised. — You are not to be hurt by anything now, and you cannot be hurt, for you know

71

the kingly defense of self-recognition sustained in spite of opinions.

As Jesus stands here accused while innocent, seeing only himself in his accusers, sustaining his own vision till the centuries do now ratify it, so this lesson assures any man who recognizes the not-guilty God in himself and stands to it, that he shall not only see the not guilty God in himself, but in all men also. And, as it was not many days after they cried, "Crucify him!" that they were pricked to the heart with regrets, so it shall not be many days after we have been accused that those who have accused shall be praising.

The pain and shame of being falsely witnessed against count for nothing to him that knows that, it being only themselves the accusers are seeing, the not guilty one will soon be reigning in glory.

It is not possible to hurt, either bodily or mentally, him that knows himself at his not guilty standing place. There he is judge and ruler and king, and what he sees is what the world must ratify.

This lesson teaches that the movements are quick between condemnation and praise for one who through self-recognition, finds the scourges of tongues and the thongs of prisons unequal to giving him pain.

For he shall be hid from the scourge of the tongue, and no weapon that is formed against him

can prosper. And his judgment shall be estab-
lished in all the earth.

The Chicago Inter-Ocean Newspaper May 19, 1895

LESSON VIII

The Day Of The Crucifixion

Mark 15:22-37

There are now said to be over two million people in the United States who believe that Schopenhauer's theory that the world that we see is our mental picture is truth.

On this principle they find disease a delusion, or mental presentation only, and not the fact of the case. On this principle they find thievery, bribery, murder, etc., are delusions, or mental presentations only, and not the facts of the case. Therefore, that great reformer, Dr. Parkhurst, of New York City, says they are following a "prodigy of systematized idiocy."

Just at hand, simultaneously with the paragraph containing Dr. Parkhurst's opinion of practical Schopenhaueritism, is a letter from one of the two million stating that after a few weeks of steady application of the mental insistence that a man's deafness was delusion and not fact he recovered his hearing faculty. Also that after a few weeks of steady insistence that a man's wish to commit suicide and his opium eating were delusions and not facts he recovered his right conduct.

Of course back of the mental factory where heterogeneous conditions are reeled there is something that is real, something that is not a mental presentation. Man is so constituted that he can live in the world of his own imagination or in the real world all the time, or part of the time, or never, at his own option.

Jesus of Nazareth knew this. He passed from seeing the best kind and the poorest kind of condition which imaginations could depict to the real country which was not built by imaginations within sixty-two days, according to the new counting, instead of within three years as according to the old count.

All his life he had realized the Taostic doctrine that "the foot treads the ground in walking; nevertheless, it is the ground not trodden on which makes up the walk." That is, he had known all his life that the world of flesh, or matter, that surrounded him was mental presentation and the world back of him was an independent fact.

"The flesh profiteth nothing."

"The kingdom of heaven cometh not by observing the material universe or the mind that spreads it out."

Understanding this he stopped his mental operation utterly and entirely. He even stopped praising God. While yet knowing the sublimest language resident in the skull of man he appreciated that to use it would swing round him on the face-to-face empyrean a world of objects and people not genuine.

The Place of the Skull

To-day's International lesson is found in Mark 15:22-37. *"And they bring him unto the place of Golgotha*, which is, being interpreted, the place of the skull."

Look at this verse from the standpoint of one who knows that this mass of materiality that enfolds us is mental presentation and that we all got our mentals from suggestions floating around from other mentals.

This makes Jesus a man who rose by the suggestions of men to the very skull place of mentality and even at the highest pitch of what intellect can do he found it crucifying or cutting off the sight of or entirely differing from fact. Therefore even the supremest teachings of mind he declined.

Intellect resides in the skull. It imagines religions, it imagines sciences, it postulates good, it postulates bad, it reasons mathematics, it devises hades, it sings hymns, it persecutes neighbors, it sets up kings, it swears and prays. But whatever it is at it is crucifying or hiding fact. One has to swing around - turn - from its creative, picturing lingos to what is real, or he must suffer and rejoice at its dictates. Jesus took the heights of intellect and experienced the interest it offers, unopiated by myrrh and unstimulated by wine. (Verse 23) He took unadulterated Calvary. It was not as if he were obliged to take it. How sublime a difference between letting the doctrines of men drag you up heights and down deeps of suffering and joy in the simpleton-like confidence that they are heaven's own decrees, and taking them all to practically prove how much they are worth, how much power they have that you may from actual experience pronounce them worthless and powerless.

Intellect has its religious promises. Those are its wine. But its religious promises are its own manufacture. They are not true. Intellect has its philosophical speculations. They are its myrrh. But they are its own manufacture whether congregated into the Golgotha of the living Dalai Lama or starting the pages of history with the enduring stoicism of Epictetus.

Led up the heights of the wise men's postulates the living Dalai Lama always is profoundly sorrowful because of the hidden fact. His eyes are on the panoramas spread forth by intellect. Led down the dungeon's path of intellect's proclamations Schopenhauer is forced to declare that evil is the gigantic god of the universe. They forget their own affirmations when high suggestions roll anguish into their lot. And they cannot help forgetting. But Jesus did not forget because he could not help himself. He forgot that he might taste man's cup once and let man know that he need not taste it. Once prove that the heights and the depths of the diapason (interval) of time are only the running of intellect, never the fact of intelligence, and he would save man the humiliation of being forever the seeming victim of nature with her object lessons of perpetual cruelty; of other men with their objections to each other's existence.

Cast Lots on His Garments

At intellect's best she imprisons the man who invented a microscope and starves the man who invents a telescope; burns Tyndall, who prints her Bibles, and calls "systematized idiocy" the healing principles of Quimby.

"And when they had crucified him they parted his garments, casting lots upon them, what every man should take." (Verse 24) The "garments" of a man are his discoveries. Scientists use the microscope now. So do religionists.

Scientists use the telescope and the Bible now. So do religionists. Scientists use the Jesus Christ God. So do the religionists when they want to praise and give thanks. They fall back on Elijah's God when they want to mow down their enemies.

No man hath yet taken the whole garment of Jesus. It is particularly stated that each man took what he could get. And the reason no man can get the whole garment or all the practical discovery of Jesus is because he will not first accept the invisible garment of nakedness of that world presented or formulated by the skull.

The discoveries of Jesus were discoveries of heaven. What he saw in heaven cast a radiance around him and made his robes so beautiful that men wanted both the radiance of heavenly power and the seamless clothing.

The same "they" who led him up Calvary tried to give him religion and philosophy to cheer his lot, namely, wine and myrrh; and afterward "they" clutched for his robes of wool, and later on "they" strove for his robes of powerfulness.

But no man cometh unto me and is me who cometh not to the Father - that which seeth not iniquity, that which createth no poorhouse or prison. Ho! Every one that is thirsty, hungry, starved, disadvantaged; in me, now, is rest from the intellect-built world; in me is heaven; I have touched God only till I am only God, So he that now cometh unto me I will in no wise cast out. He that receiveth me receiveth him that sent me. He that receiveth me as I am receiveth all my garments.

He hath my powerfulness, he hath my everlasting robes. Sinners and righteous men, one and the same in having the fact of heaven hidden by intellect, I have no science to offer, I have no religion to offer. At their best they are the presentments of the skull, that imitation of intelligence, shadow of authority. While the sciences of intellect spread their proclamations on the ethers with their explanations of things that have no explanation of which intellect can divine, there must be darkness and light, death and life alternating to mark the alternating mentals of the skull.

With Two Thieves

"But there are no alternations in me. At evening time it is light. In me is no darkness at all. I am the rest of man from time and pain and I change not. I am the protection of man from man and I fail never. I am the safety of man from shame and fear and I sleep not. I am the king of the Jews. For the Jews speak of their king my God, and I am he, I and the father are one." (Verse 36)

"And with him they crucify two thieves." Who crucified them? "They" of the skull. How are men made into thieves? Are they thieves? "He was numbered with the transgressors." Who numbers Jesus as a transgressor? "They" of the skull. Imaginations of the skull, which at its topmost hath no power only such as is imagined.

Was there any difference between the two thieves and Jesus? Intrinsically, no; they represent man forgetting his godhood, and he represents man remembering his godhood.

"And they that passed by railed on him, mocking. He saved others; himself he cannot save. He that keepeth his knowledge of his own divinity is already secure. He that keepeth his knowledge of other men's divinity secureth them to themselves. And at high noon there was darkness over all the land for they of the skull had full sway." (Verse 33)

Till 3 o'clock in the afternoon science and religion held high carnival.

This part of the crucifixion scene is now going on. When you hear the wail of the poverty stricken, the defeated, the so-called criminals, and the helpless, to whom it verily seems as if the intellect would reign forever, with its proud sciences of nothingness, this is Jesus taking the wail of mankind who have forgotten their godhood in Golgotha. "Let us see whether Elias will come to take him down." No, the Elias of doctrine is very, very wonderful, but it is still the science of safety by reasonable explanations of God. When the intellect has full sway we always notice that nothing reasonable appeals. The hour hath arrived when Jesus Christ is his own appeal. Elias, the good metaphysician of the past, cannot take the people down from the wailing world of the mentals. The present Jesus Christ taketh a way of appeal that cannot be explained.

"And Jesus cried with a loud voice, and gave up the ghost." Thus he took this people's cry. When you hear the people crying out that they do not know what to believe among the multitudinous sciences and religions of this day you may know that they are giving up confidences in mentals and giving up that mind, in whose ghostly regions outward conditions are first manufactured. How near the heavenly garments of power and glory are the people when they give up confiding their minds to the changing formulas of science and

religion, whose explanations have never hit the facts of heaven and earth and never can.

The God that is, is not explainable. Jesus Christ is God. Pin it as a star in the darkness of today's proud sciences that Jesus Christ is the unexplainable God.

And yet in his name shall the gentiles trust, and yet to his name shall the nations come.

The earth mind shall reel to and fro like a drunken man, but it shall come to pass in that day that whosoever shall call on the name of the Lord shall be secure.

The Chicago Inter-Ocean Newspaper May 26, 1895

LESSON IX

At The Tomb

Mark 16:1-8

"With carecloth and band
  For the grave we arrayed him;
But, oh, he is gone
  From the place where we laid him."
Goethe's Faust

Is there any doubt about final events and un-
prejudiced history bringing to light every
prominent person's actual motives and accom-
plishments? Who first declared in this country
that disease is a mental concept, and not a fact?
What did General Grant actually do for his country? What is the "unwritten story of Lincoln's
assassination?" Answers to these questions will
stand out on the next century's pages of literature
in all their bald, bold differences from the way we,
as a people, insist on having them printed now.

A certain magazine, commenting on the current literature of this age as reporting

transactions, declares that "if the college corre-
spondents (most of whom depend on their
newspaper writing for their daily bread) send in
calm, scholarly discussions, their matter is not
printed; but if they dash off the charges of this,
that, and the other against somebody or something, the least substantial statement is printed
eagerly. Why did the statement in the *New York
Herald* of May 19, concerning the canals on
"Mars," rouse scarcely an amoeba of confidence?
Because so many fake stories are told that though
this was one of the most interesting items of modern times, if it should prove true, it was believed to
be only an insubstantial piece of sensational writing.

How did current opinion settle the disappear-
ance of Jesus from the sepulcher? "His disciples
came by night and stole him away." This was the
public pacification *pro tem.*

The man or the woman whose actual motives
and character are hidden by misrepresentations
that play on the Pilate streak that runs through
human mind is sure to shine all the brighter and
stronger for the temporary eclipse which lies com-
pose.

> *"We are the work of Providence,*
> *And more the battle's loss*
> *May profit those who lose*
> *Than victory advantage those who win."*

Clouds Often Obscure Greatness

It is one of the laws of the sun that it shall be hidden by darkness now and then. It is one of the laws of the great of the world that they shall be hidden by the enmity of the small and mean for some season. But the sun is an unkillable light. Greatness is an unhidable splendor. There is no destroying Christ.

Faraday's servant dropped a silver cup into a pan of acid and it promptly disappeared. The servant whimpered and whined at the supposed irrevocable loss. But Faraday dropped a neutral into the acid and the undestroyed silver came up to be made into the same cup.

Oh, whimperer over thine own sorrow-bitten life, knowest thou not better than to play the dull head, when the neutral to sorrow is in the universe, close to thy touch? Happiness is the unkillable silver of thy destiny, however crucified by the acids of sorrow. Drop in the neutrals and take it up with not even the memory of the acids about it, "They shall forget misery as waters that pass away." They took the wonderful Jesus and hid him behind the very worst that their acids could do. But he understood neutrals.

"From three days' sleep in death,
As the sun has risen."

These last six months are the record of one man on this globe who boldly undertook to heal all the nations of men, born and unborn, of the hurting clutches of the "Prince of the world."

Is it not now understood that we mean the opposite of the merciful when we say "prince of this world?" Do we not mean that movement of phenomenal life whereby the big fishes eat the little ones and the human sharks eat the fishes? Is that a merciful movement which enables chief priests by accident of opportunity to imprison an innocent man because he is in favor with the masses and brings a kinder message from the law of life than they bring? Is that a merciful movement which hangs a John Brown?

Secret Doctrine of Jesus' Life Work

That movement of hurting is the movement of the Prince nature of this world. It was against the hurting principles of nature and man that Jesus arrayed himself.

The Prince of this world cometh and findeth nothing like himself in me.

Now, the last act of the hurting principle, whether practiced by man when he has gotten his fellow men down so that their starved bones lie bleaching on the grass plains of America, or practiced by the sea as it folds the wrecked shipload, is when the life is hidden, the form not seen to breathe.

"Now," says the hurting principle, "I have you!" But Jesus had the absolute neutral to every movement of the hurting principle from first to last. Even the sealed sepulcher was nothing to him. "Destroy me, O hurting opposite to my kindness, and I will appear again. Cover me with rocks deep in the earth and I will arise again."

Now the secret doctrine contained in the life work of Jesus is openly heralded, but who catches that secret? The secret doctrine is the actual power of the Jesus man who dissolved all flesh nature in divine fact as fast as flesh nature arrived on him, to set all living things entirely free from even the least encroachment of the hurting principle. The secret doctrine is the actual power of the Jesus man who dissolved all hurts as fast as they came to him, to set all living things free from the Prince of this world.

The secret doctrine is the actual power of the one who has dissolved rheumatism in himself by divine substance to cure all who have rheumatism by their accepting his cure as their cure.

Help Offered the Unsuccessful

The man who has undertaken an enterprise which is not successful may be healed of the unsuccessful movement in his enterprise by accepting the unsuccessfulness of Jesus of Nazareth as having embodied in itself all the unsuccessfulness with which the hurting principle is capable of touching humanity.

This healing of the hurts of the world by embodying all those hurts in one bitter mass and neutralizing them forever is the whole ministry of Jesus. It is what he meant in Galilee, Samaria, Perea, Idumea, Caesarea Philippi. He stood in Jerusalem and swallowed hate and neutralized it, for it was a movement of a prince of this world. Jesus stands for the all-kind. The prince stands for the all-cruel. And the kingdom of the all-kind shall be from sea to sea and from the river to the ends of the earth. And the reign of the all-kind begins in any man's life when he accepts the healing office of an all-kind man, who, by defeating hate on an entirely divine plan, made himself a healer of hate everywhere.

Now, these six months of lessons have all turned on that fact of the meaning of Jesus Christ. Whoever has missed that healing office through missing this healer's offer, is, without doubt, still crying with misfortune of some kind.

It was Jesus who demonstrated that there is no reality in evil, no other substance but God, and that the prince of this world as a hurting principle is nothing at all.

Today's Bible lesson touches the historic movement when the two Marys came to anoint a body and found it gone. (Mark 16:1-8)

The Mary Disposition Defined

The Mary disposition is that soft quality in us which takes it for granted that the hurting principle is the victorious governor of this life; with it we rejoice when pain lets go a moment, weep when it gets hold again, anoint and tend in faithful fondness all plants and children, men and dogs, but with it we never were known to look for an uncrucified living Power. We weep when things look down, we smile when they look up, but with our

Mary nature we never sit on the right hand of life saying: "life reigns,"

We, with our softly-kind Mary disposition, doubled and twisted into us, never go toward a glorified triumph of health saying: "Health reigns." We are doubled and twisted into soft kindness to pour arnica on wounds until some wonderful man tells us that pain and death are delusions. Some man told the Marys that there are never any wounds to dress. There is never any hurt, sicklied form to handle with Mary tenderness. It is the untaught two-Mary system which keeps us forever mauling and moaning around in hospitals. But it is the softness of the Mary kindness that first hears the angelic message: *"He is not here."* (Verse 5)

It is truly to the kind-hearted of the world that the tidings of the unreality of obstacles, comes first. (Verse 4)

It is truly to the Mary quality that is searching around for the best thing to do, the last thing to do, early and late, that the man who hath a wonderful character (called in verse 5 a "garment") and who sits on the right of doctrine and health (as verse 5) first says, with a voice that causes the Mary quality to spring: *"Be not affrighted; ye seek Jesus of Nazareth, which was crucified; he is risen; he is not here; behold the place where they laid him."*

Love of Self Teaches Love of Others

There was never a Mary yet that discovered a risen Christ till she was told by the Angel man that he was not dead. Mary expects a dead man. It is her ministering nature which leads her to the tomb to comfort herself by doing something or other. When she is told that there is no reality in death, no hindrance in matter, she is amazed and keeps silent for a season that she may tell the world what the wonderful being told her in secret.

Here, in verse 8, is one principle which goes straight against all church and school, and home instruction that we have ever had. It knocks ethics down at its first statement, but picks them up again at its second.

"Neither said they anything to any men; for they were afraid."

This teaches man to love himself first and foremost, and then only can he love his neighbor; to be good to himself first and foremost, and only then can he be good to his neighbors; to work for himself first and foremost, and only then can he work for his neighbors. The sun conserves caloric before it has caloric to dispense. *"God so loved the world that he gave his only begotten son."* But he had to beget the son before he had him to give. The whole splendor of the thirty years' life of Jesus was given to conserving his divinity. He dispensed divinity enough in sixty-two days, after such conservation, to electrify a world.

Shakespeare says: "Love thyself last," but Jesus Christ taught, *"Love thyself first," "Father, glorify thyself through me." "Glorify me."* Then when the glory was intense enough he shed it like a sun on the solar system planet by planet.

All principles have their legitimate outcomes. The church dogma, of give to, do for, work for, yield all, to neighbor man, has for its credit on the pages of judgment a wonderful title. That title is the legitimate fruit of its principle of, give, give, give. It is a title we are all familiar with. It is "Superlative Selfishness." The selfishness of mankind forms the pessimistic theme of poetry, essay, sermon, prayer, and at the central focus of modern church insistence of "give," they have a leaning tower as a perpetual emblem of the stretch and strain of the dislocated dogma of doing our best.

Selfishness the Outcome of Sacrifice

Taking the principle of giving everything we have to others, doing all the time for others, loving others first, has for its outcome selfishness in the whole world. For it makes an everlasting rebellion in the hearts of all who practice it, because they are inadequate to meet the demands upon them. So they lean; they do not stand upright. The tower of Pisa is the world's standing monument to the effect of taking an ethical position with our language which the conduct cannot follow.

The two Marys kept what they had to themselves in fear till their presence was so charged up with power that they were convincing energies.

They told no man by the way. Their secret motto was: "I love myself. I am good to myself, I work for myself." And this self was the Jesus Christ in their hearts.

"Fear" in the Scriptures means single-eyed. One-purposed, single-purposed. "They" were intensely single-pointed. It is to the heart's own divine secret that we must first do honor. For at the heart of us all is the Jesus Christ power unkillable. "To love thyself last" is to tell everybody about Jesus Christ, but be no Jesus Christ in thyself; and so we strain and struggle to make other people do the right ways, learn the right doctrines, hear about healing miracles and everlasting powers, but our first duty was to stand upright on our own feet and acknowledge the unkillable glory within our own living heart and do nothing for anybody till the bursting splendor of our risen powers makes for itself a new order of ministering, with convincible fire enough for a whole world's healing. When this new order of ministry strikes on the world, the tower of Pisa will crumble and fall, for there cannot be an emblem of a principle that no longer holds any sway. The preaching power of the Marys was gendered by milling in silence what the wonderful man had told her. She milled it for her own glory, and by so doing she glorified the world. Come out straight in the acknowledgment that it is for the glorification of the unspoilable Jesus Christ. In thine own heart thou art working, and no fruits like the title of "superla-

94

tive selfishness" can be thine through inadequacy to meet the multitudinous demands of a world — for it is inadequacy that compels that title. But there is a power of ministry equal to meeting every demand, and that comes by standing straight up and declaring that the Jesus Christ in our own heart is what we love first, and are doing all that we are doing for.

The Chicago Inter-Ocean Newspaper June 2, 1895

LESSON X

The Road To Emmaus

Luke 24:13-32

Jesus Christ is the indwelling light of which the Quakers tell. Bancroft, in a noble chapter on Quakerism, says that "that light is a reality, and, therefore, in its freedom the highest revelation of truth, it is kindred with the spirit of God, and, therefore, in its purity should be listened to as the guide."

"Too late I loved thee, O beauty of ancient days, yet ever new!" said Augustine. *"And lo! thou wert within, and I abroad searching for thee!"*

Today's Bible lesson tells of two men on their way to Emmaus in deep sorrow of heart because they had no Christ Jesus. (Luke 24:13-32) Luke, the writer of this gospel addresses it to Theophilus. Learned commentators have been for ages trying to find out who Theophilus was. The indwelling light shows that it was not to one man, but to the love of God in all men that this gospel was told.

Luke wrote the Acts of the Apostles and addressed that book also to Theophilus, or the love chord in all hearts. This love chord is the inner light. So today's lesson is addressed to all people who have lost track of their indwelling light; who feel depressed because of not having plain evidences today, this week, this month, this year

Luke says that it is when two negative ideas get the upper hands in our mentality that we have the depression of logs. Learned commentators are still beating their heads over who those two men were who were so mournfully conversing about the crucified Christ and the improbability of his having come to life again. But Luke is writing interiorly to all hearts in all time. The love of God is born with man. The two ideas which cause mourning over a lost light are common ideas which all men have who have once felt the inner light. Luke calls one of them "Cleopas" in verse 13. This Cleopas is the habit of remembering evil events. It is a name taken from the muse of history (Clio). Even if we admit with some writers that it comes from "Alpheus," it still means "succession" or one event succeeding another.

The other man who is so silent, but who makes such a good listener, has utterly puzzled the good Bible students, who understood so much Hebrew, Greek, and Latin construction that they have no time to watch the indwelling light. But those who are not so interested in the letters of these gospels as in their spiritual power, know by the way the Jesus Christ presence so promptly explains Moses and the prophets, that the other man, who is so silent, represents the prophetic principle in mankind.

Prophecy Listening to History

So history gets to detailing the dark, the negative side of events, for the most part, with just a slight sprinkling of light streaks, as in verses 22 and 23, where Cleopas, the historian, says that certain women do insist that Jesus is not dead. And prophecy listens to history, for prophecy is dependent upon history, *"For,"* says Solomon, *"the thing that hath been, it shall be."* If the earth goes on this sun's orbit she will certainly get between Mars and Sol again, and we can figure to a second when she hits the rim. And if (Nicolas Camille) Flammarion and (Giovanni) Schiaparelli keep on in the same orbit they are now going they are destined to hit the translation of those canals on Mars which are now said to look exactly like the old Hebrew name for the moveless, changeless God.

The foot of a giant pre-histories (this is not a complete sentence). a great rib and elbow. Noticing a perturbation an astronomer predicts the future discovery of another globe in space. Watching the history of past civilizations where the people let all the wealth creep into the hands of a few it is easy enough to predict for the United States, taking notice, however, of the fact that past nations had no terrible factor at work against inequality, like that one which is managing in our age, prophecy must set up a counter figuring this time.

Rome was not walking with the Jesus Christ factor but America is counting on that mighty principle. And this chapter of Luke proclaims that that people who reckon up misfortunes for a future based on misfortunes and a past are "fools and slow of heart," if they forget that just at the moment when all the world is afraid history is about to repeat herself she cannot repeat herself, for she has another kind of people to deal with, namely, a multitude who can lay their prayers on the omnipotent Christ.

Influence of the Indwelling Light

This scene en-route to Emmaus details how people must talk who have felt the indwelling light. They must not talk like people who have ignored it. Augustine was searching and travelling for the light through books and countries. So are our learned ones today. Historians tremble for our future. Prophets are very silent, and when they do speak they tell of dreadful things, but there's a grand difference stealing along on our human march in this year of our Lord one thousand eight hundred and ninety-five. *"While they communed together Jesus himself was drawing nigh."* (Verse 16)

The learning of this world while making its calculations from the past, is always forgetting that we have another factor now to deal with.

Even those who dare felt the light burning at their own heart center forget to pick out the points in history which made conditions for a different movement this time when the same elements of human nature are aroused.

"Their eyes were holden that they should not know him." (Verse 16)

So it is now time for the Jesus Christ light to shine on talkative history and quiet prophecy. "When beginning at Moses and all the prophets he expounded unto them the promise" to Eve as in Gen. 3:15; the promise to Abraham as in Gen. 22:18; the prophecies which read as though things were already past which were ages ahead, as Isaiah 9:6-7; Malachi 3:l; Ezekiel 34:23, Isaiah 43:4-5.

This lesson shows what powerful adepts the ancients were with their ideas. They insisted that a child should be born with a mighty knowledge of the divine presence. And their idea came true. Then they insisted that he would be crucified by envy; and their idea came to fruitage. They insisted that he should rise from the dead, and he did. Therefore he saith unto them, "ought not Christ to have suffered these things, and to enter into his glory?"

So his name carries a conscious knowledge of independence of race hypnotisms. He did it on purpose. He knew what he knew. He knew what his name would do. It is the only name of any man or God that is not hypnotic. It is the only name that opens the gate of every man's mind and wakes him up as a lion from this earth stupor.

Traveling on with the heavy paws of old adepts of Palestine and India heavy on our destinies, we get poor, old, sick, dead, age after age, because they said: "This is the law of life." But to the glory of them be it said they promised one independent man to come on this globe who should understand their stupid adeptship for what it was worth, and take their paws of language off himself.

This lesson has for its golden text: "He opened to us the Scriptures." And "He" is the indwelling Christ. Does not this doctrine of the stupefying power of prophecies and histories talking themselves over and over get itself exposed with the swing of one stream of the light on their nonsense?

The Past and Future are Burned
To this Christ Jesus there is no law of man.

Man's words count for nothing. He stretches himself up out of the old saying that what has been it shall be. He puts his hot wisdom forth from his own heart and shows history that it was all made by adepts in formulating postulates, but that he shall burn up their postulates. He shows prophecy better than to work any longer on the old maxims, for he has burned maxims alive and the dispensation of independent knowledge has dawned. *"And their eyes were opened and they knew him."* (Verse 31)

So it is clear that we are apt to get to rehearsing the events of a material past and to looking forward to a future bred by a past. We get discouraged when we think of the past and we have no happy hope from our past experiences to light our future with. These two ideas are the two men of this section, taken spiritually or mentally, or metaphysically. One is Cleopas — historic musings; the other is the muse of futurity, wrapped closely around with listening wonder and awe. The muse Polyhymnia might serve as the name of the unhopeful spirit that rises within us all when we reckon on our own futures as judged by our own pasts. But, that man being nameless in the gospels, this muse cannot truly name him.

This section of gospel instruction declares that we cannot count on what is to come as in any sense like what has been if we now know the name of that deathless fire of wisdom in our own hearts. The past is burned. The future also is burned. "Did not our hearts burn within us?" said the two men. The absolute new life, unrelated to the past and unheralded by prophecy, now opens.

He openeth unto us the Scriptures — the wonderful scriptures of the new heaven and the new earth. They form the language which no man readeth save he that hath held fast the name. (Revelation 2:13 and 17)

This young man Jesus well knew that he was carrying out the ideas of the past in order that none of us need carry out any past ideas. It is a well-known law of metaphysics that most people are carrying out other people's ideas of them. Unless a child touches some principle which sets him free he is sure to carry out some person's idea of him, which once having been hurled at him plated him into a copper vest of necessity.

The Egyptians taught how powerful is somebody's — "It Is."

The Shattering of the Powerful "It Is"

Well for the child who has been taught to stand up and says "It is not!" Is it not written that if a child is black-skinned it is bound to stay so? Some mighty adept in ideas put forth an "it is so." But some other mighty adept in ideas may put forth an "it is not so!" that will shatter it all to pieces. This is Christ entering into his glory. "I will do as they said," he agreed.

And I will close up the dispensation of man as under bondage to adepts. And so it has come to pass that no man, however strong with his hypnotic ideas, can make anybody do or say a single thing he tries to make them do if they have the independence-brooding name Jesus Christ in their heart.

The future is hypnotized by the past if the independent principle is not brought into the movement. Jesus understood this and struck the downward trend of history a great blow. For he took the old adepts' prophecies of his suffering and carried them out while yet saying that any instant he could swing out of their clutches.

The Chicago Inter-Ocean Newspaper June 9, 1895

LESSON XI

Fisher Of Men

John 21:4-17

The animus of night meditation paints itself on the face and in the home very early in the morning? — Or speedily.

Stop a minute and take account of stock. When you waken in the night, or the moment you are silent and alone, what sort of meditation seizes you? There is a religion which has for one of its assurances that if we have a habit of meditating on the nature of celestial beings we shall ourselves show a luminousness of skin like the celestials and also have a smile and touch similar to their indescribable salutations.

The doctrine of fishing is the doctrine of seizures by skilled labor. That is, accomplishing things by scientific processes. "The work of the fisher is a work of arts and skill rather than force," says Peloubet. When Jesus found Peter and John they were skilled, materialists. They knew exactly how to spear the little helpless water denizens and stamp their heads into the sand with utter disregard of the eternal protest walking with them just back of their hearts.

Jesus told them he would show them a new kind of fishing business, namely, mental meditations, which would haul in new personal characters, powers, influences. *"Immediately they left their nets and followed him."* He kept his word, for, after a very few days, they could do astounding things by their minds alone, without pill or plaster or surgeons' tools or visible aide-de-camp of any sort.

The new fishing tackle was identically the same that the adepts of India were then using. They called it "meditation." This, as we all know, means silent mental fishing. If when, we waken in the night watches, we go to meditating on how badly John has acted or how unkind Lilly is or how homely we are or how shall we get ahead of the shoe string syndicate, we shall fish in quite promptly hard wrinkles, feeble eyes, black teeth, depressions in finance.

Fallacy of Unpleasant Meditation

Knowing the importance of skill and intelligence in the new style of fishing Jesus was teaching them, he told them to abjure such tackling meditations. *"If any man would come after me let him deny himself,"* he said imperatively. He perceived that they were meditating sometimes on processes for getting ahead of each other. This is a universal human tendency. This tendency is a man's "himself." Let him deny such meditations. Ignore them. Stop them. Have nothing to do with them. They will "very early in the morning" show their marks on the face and body and affairs.

John, the tenth disciple, counting from last to first, found out that there are four subjects of meditation which make up a mental fishing tackle to drag decrepit faculties into sight.

First, "what do people think of me?" Second, the sex principle. Third, "how shall I perform so as to be something or somebody?" Fourth, "my poverty or riches and how to alter them." "Bad tackling," he said.

David found that he was inclined to take up these four subjects and harp on them every time he opened his eyes in the night, and so one day he resolved to hold his mental machinery to one subject only. That should be the divine being and his works. *I will meditate on thee in the night patches. I will meditate of thy works.*

Simon Magus resolutely persisted in whispering into the responsive ethers of the earth till he fished up by that whispering hook, the levitation of his body. The whisper he used read something like this: "Breathe into me, O mother earth, and I will breathe back to thee; and lift me high as the stars and I will come back to thee again."

Solomon insisted that we could fish in quite a good state of affaire by wearing a ribbon around our neck with the words "mercy and truth" written on it. The story of the Ephesian wrestler who wore a strip of writing bound around his ankle is well known. Without that metaphysical hook he failed. With it he succeeded.

Wisdom and Discretion

Solomon once wrote that "wisdom and discretion" were excellent words to swing around in his own mind like fish lines in the night watches, instead of the subjects that had heretofore taken such extraordinary hold of his mind. He promised that these two hooks would draw in life to the soul for other people as they had for him.

A certain ancient Brahman declared that "friendship" was an excellent word to swing around and hold still and otherwise mentally maneuver with. This metaphysical activity was what the fishermen of Galilee went into after their service of physical nets and lines.

The Jesus Christ power which they finally achieved on the mental plane was as successful with them as their skill in draughting and killing fishes had formerly been. But as the first circuit of stamping the life out of water herds for the sake of their own support came to a sudden end, so their ability to swing and flourish sentences and paragraphs came to a sudden halt. This incompetency to earn their living by metaphysical activities is the place where today's lesson begins. (John 21:4-17)

They had been hanging and, dragging and maneuvering all night, but nothing had come of it. The mind gets just as barren of achievements as the hands and vocal chords if mankind persist in using the mind with the supposition that it is by swinging and pulling thoughts about, that life, health, strength, and intelligence are supported. These things are the gift of the Jesus Christ presence in this universe. This lesson explains that skilled labor with the ears, eyes, nostrils, tongue, teeth, etc., without knowledge of the mind principle that lies back of them, comes in its own time to a dead halt. The eyes want to see, the hands drop the knife and fork, the tongue falters. With the knowledge of how every movement can be revived and renewed by thoughts, the powers and faculties last much longer and are much stronger. Mr. William T. Stead was astonished to find "intelligent people" in the United States who had improved and supplemented their muscular energies and cured their bodies by the new style of thoughts called Christian Science reasoning. He did not interview those who have come to the limits of all that metaphysical reasonings or thought maneuvering can do, who are as badly off mentally and physically as those who never heard of the science, with the bare exception of believing that there is no need of being in the science

States of Unsuccessful Planners Typified
Successful fishers whose inward confidence that there is no need of their being unsuccessful, is

that line in them which brings forth fruits, and not indeed their brave struggles either with thoughts or surgery or pills or syndicates.

This lesson teaches that the inner certainty of the metaphysically taught is a sure bringer of what is expected.

Some of these lessons are manifestly for the closed metaphysician who cannot manage his destiny, but who terribly needs help. He can read his situation and his cure. When he has nothing else to go by, these chapters will show him exactly how to steer himself or manage his destiny.

Did not last Sunday's section plainly teach that when a man takes the Christ Jesus factor into his life he has stepped out of what was written in his fate, and there is nobody who can say that he is going to be under the consequences of his past thoughts or deeds? Did not one man show how history was burned, and the other show how prophecy is burned also?

One man in history had a name. The other silent man, waiting for history to repeat itself miserably in him, had no name, for he was unwritten futurity.

So today's lesson takes people who are toiling at their meditations, expecting them to work just as well after they have struck the Jesus Christ note in Christian Science as they did before they knew it. But when we see the palsied, half-blind, lame, poverty-stricken crew performing ineffectual gymnastics with their thought wings, let it be known that it only means that their all night's useless fishing is closing up the dispensation of seizures of things by thoughts.

They are closed to the strike of miraculous proceedings in their behalf with which they have had apparently nothing whatsoever to do.

Notice that these fishermen had nothing to do about that fire and food and wisdom that saluted them. That is, nothing moving. Their thoughts were useless, their hands were useless. All they had left was their unmoving inner certainty that they would not be in such misfortune if they could touch the right spring. The more they thought the less they knew. The more they worked the less they accomplished.

Philosophy of Being Moveless

Jesus had formerly taught them to keep still under such circumstances, and let the moveless certainty be all there was of them. Had he not kept so still, when everything and every body failed him that Pilate marveled? So when rowing does no good, stop rowing. When thinking Christian Science thoughts does no good, stop thinking. The inner certainty that there is a way out, a way of freedom, a way of glad help, is enough. It has its morning time just as much as the active fishery had its, whether on the material circuit of self-help or on the mental circuit of self-help.

"When the morning was now come, Jesus stood on the shore." That word "Jesus" here stands for

113

dispensation. The old had closed. For the first time in their lives the great workers were still. The first movement of mind after a pause in its activity is overwhelmingly powerful. A certain adept in mental notions keeps utterly still with his mind allowing not a thought to exercise itself on the clear surface, and then he says, "I shall do so and so." And he does. (Verse 6)

But this lesson goes beyond the stirring of a right thought on the limpid water of a well-stilled mind, and shows how when eating and drinking and clothing and warming ourselves by right thoughts metaphysically we are on the labor line of science just as much as when striking with hammers on stones and sewing of cloth with needles for our daily bread.

For Jesus showed them that all their adeptship in thoughts counted for nothing in his kingdom. (Verse 8)

Peter was clean, naked of ideas, and so got the first treatment. (Verse 7)

On the clear, quiet surface of the lake, the skies and trees and cathedrals of the country cast their forms in exactness. So on the clear mind of Peter, first to cast himself loose from the high dogmas of the science of skilled meditations, the heavenly man and the heavenly food and the heavenly power first cast their perfect forms.

The Threefold Perception of Peter

Commentators perceive that John uses three different words in the Greek for "love." So Peter is aware that first he cares nothing for material possessions secured by right thoughts, and will do no more thinking to bring them. If they come not by reason of his own splendid being, he will let them go by. (Verse 15)

And secondly, he is aware that he cares nothing for friends gathered around him by season of the attractive energies of his flashing speculative philosophies. What comrades come not to the shining presence he is on this earth, he will let go by. (Verse 16)

And thirdly, he perceives that he is too wonderful in his own glorious body to care to work miracles by managing high reasonings about truth and error, man and destiny. What miracles shine not by themselves on his vision may stay away. (Verse 17)

The first perception makes him a mighty provider. The second perception makes him a mighty informer. The third perception makes him a heavenly helper. It is here called "feeding sheep and lambs" by simply existing as the roses perfume June gardens by simply being there.

The glory of the Jesus Christ man is that on his native nature all heavenly powers and provisions are reflected, nothing else. And forth from his native nature shine visions, friendship, with helping abilities, and all the kind gifts of a good

unknown to the man of action on the physical or
metaphysical plane.

Lesson in "Be Still and Know"

The ordinary interpretations of these texts
have been harped on for now 1800 years. Let us
quote one explanation from Peloubet's excellent
notes, on page 172, verse 10: "Feed my sheep; tend
or shepherd my sheep;" a different word from the
one translated feed in the previous verse. It in-
cludes watching, feeding, leading, guarding.

This may absorb the attention of Greek and
Hebrew intellects, but does not indeed touch the
heavenly fact the Jesus Christ story prints on the
limpid surface of any mind that having once seen
how unprofitable are all the whirring systems of
civilized and uncivilized man, lets them utterly
alone and permits the Jesus Christ presence to do
its own way.

See how marvelous were the provisions of
heaven for the fishermen of Galilee. Shall the everlasting One do less for men when they heed
practically the great command, "Be still and
know?" All heaven waits here to print its changeless splendors on the clear, stir-less mind of the
free "me," wherever it may be found.

And heavenly ministries spring forth without
struggling from him that hath the kingdom of
heaven stamped on the stir-less deeps of his world-
free soul. Whether anybody has practiced this
lesson's directions or not, this is what it means. By
the other ways we certainly have counted many

weary years. By this way it was promised that this heavenly splendor of one man's obedience to it should flash like the lightning from east into west.

And surely the lightning does not take 1800 years to spring from horizon to horizon with its ministry of light.

The Chicago Inter Ocean Newspaper June 16, 1895

Lesson Xll

Missing

Luke 24:27-29

Lesson XIII

Review

Expose a sensitized photographic plate to the sky there will after a time be imaged upon it stars which the largest telescope cannot reveal.

Sensitize mind by stopping its thoughts and then expose it to the absolute and eternal facts in this universe. Such hidden glories in the inspired writings and such matchless intentions on the part of Jesus of Nazareth will become visible to that mind that it will be necessary to shut it up in prison or crowd it back out of sight if it tells its discoveries.

As instance Socrates with his sensitized plate catching principles which ordinary plates declared would pervert the youth of Athens. And Plato, sold as a slave for discovering that matter is mental caravansary and Luther, chased with threats of martyrdom for finding the fourth star in the night sky of divine science, namely, the redemptive energy of confidence in God. And, now, whoever sees that it is true that this world may be utterly relieved of foolishness and ignorance of this world in the spirit of his own understanding let whoever sees that himself may be free from foolishness by the fact, be anathema!

But there are deep truths in the night skies of science as there are many splendid stars beyond the telescopes; the fly makes a sound tramping over a plate glass window, the odors of the roses chant hymns to the grass blades under their thorns, and the spirit of man at its highest exposure is capable of making all the foolishness and sordidness of humanity actually nothing at all in all men's life.

Let the world refuse to believe that there are stars which no telescope can point out, let the world refuse to believe that the fly sounds his moccasins on the tinted ceiling, let the world refuse to believe that it need not study out or work out its own redemption from stupidity and failure, the majestic fact will still gleam on the ethers of eternity that the cure of ignorance has been all wrought out once for the world. Let the world still hold on to its belief that the Divine Presence asks martyrdom of mankind, the glad fact will still remain that all martyrdom is self-imposed, and that Jesus of Nazareth was not being martyred to teach other men how to be brave but was closing up the dispensation of foolishness and failure for all this world.

The Name and Power of the Absolute
The golden text of this review lesson tells the solid theme of the last three months: "Looking

unto Jesus the author and finisher of our faith."
There is a name and power of the absolute and
eternal. One that no man knoweth saving he that
receiveth It. One name and the power that went in
that name was once so well understood by an Ori-
ental sage that whoever pronounced the sage's
name felt immediately some of his power which he
had caught from the divine themes that he medi-
tated upon. Even the clothing of one alive with
spiritual themes has spiritual reviving in it. Did
not Paul's aprons and handkerchiefs cure the sick?
There is one church that knows enough to select
its pastors of flocks, not for their oratorical abilities but for the mesmeric spells they are adept in
casting over multitudes.

It is not the actual acting of some noted imper-
sonators, but the subtle enchantments of their
liberated spirit that hushes or convulses audi-
ences. Whatever it is they have done with
themselves, the aroma of it is powerful to do their
will among men, as Peter could dissolve sickness
with his far reaching shadow.

What was it that Jesus of Nazareth did with
himself that his voice made men forget to arrest
him at the risk of their lives, or permitted men to
arrest him, and nothing could interfere with this
choice? What did he do with himself that his clothing dispensed quickening vigor? What did he do
with himself that his name through all time
should convey all the intelligence and life and
inspiration of all the Divine Presence in the uni-

verse? What did he do with himself that he had all faith from alpha to omega and his faith is so sufficient now for all who live that they need have no faith in him or his name, yet shall be the whole office of faith, be performed for them that speak his name? *"Looking unto Jesus the author and finisher of our faith."* Heb. 12:2.

If this profound redemptive scheme, exactly as stated in the four gospels, be no delusive chimera of some author's imagination, then all this urging of men to have faith in God, before God will do anything for them has kept men from God, rather than drawn them toward him.

Today's review of the constantly offered theme of free grace shows that the Orientalist whose name could convey freedom from the drowning power of water was a forerunner of one to follow whose name should convey freedom from the heavy yokes of faith laid on the necks of all men as their only chance for life, health, peace, intelligence, inspiration, hope and heaven.

Faith Only Necessary for Miracle

In the *Andover Review* for June 1880, it tells how the Orient, from whence our faith yoke came to us, they teach that it is true we can so train our faith energy that it can cause a sardine's head to work miracles. The same faith put into the Divine Presence will cause the Divine Presence to work miracles. Neither the sardine's head nor the Divine Presence will work miracles unless we put that faith into them. What difference can be made on the bare lines of reason between such receptacles of faith? Why should a man take the energizing quality he calls faith and charge up either a sardine's head or a hypnotic presence with working efficiency? Why should he not charge up himself and be himself the engine of performance he wants the visible sardine or the invisible Divinity to be?

Jesus of Nazareth took the whole sphere of faith and glorified himself with it. His great purpose was self-glorification. His self was his God and his God was his self. *"He that hath seen me hath seen the Father."*

It is under the law of sin and death that a mind must exercise itself with hot faith before divine kindness will arrive. But the law of the spirit of life is "Christ Jesus maketh me free from the law of sin and death." Last Sunday's lesson taught that the inspiration of the spirit is an imbuement to them that rest, or tarry in relief of all responsibility of miracles. (Luke, 24:49)

It taught inspiration is the gift of the divine self of mind when mind is relieved of obligation to do great things to prove its religion.

The Jesus Christ office is the undoing of obligation to work miracles, and that relief causes mind to spread its subtle spells of power entirely round the globe. (Luke 24:47) It is the relieved mind that has the enchantment of free grace on the wings. Neither to explicit around nor worry for themselves were the Jesus Christ men to practice.

125

This relief made them the miracle workers of a shining point in history. *"Tarry ye in Jerusalem till ye be endued with power from on high."* (Luke 24:48)

The lessons of the last three months have perpetually emphasized the principle of vicarious atonement. They have shown that the hurry of martyrs and the worry of their followers and believers will never get man back into the fortress of his own power, will cure of the vast delusions now built up by religion and science.

What a test of relief from the responsibility of working miracles, is that about tarrying at Jerusalem, which means tarrying at minding our own business and letting other people alone till the radiance of the divine spell-worker performs its own ministry through us.

What a test of relief from struggling to believe in the invisible spread of a God of some kind, who will let us miserably perish, if we do not believe in him, is the golden text, "Looking unto Jesus the author and finisher of our faith."

Doubt at its coldest cannot chill the grandeur of the Holy Spirit, at its office of enduing us with its power. "There is none that can deliver out of my hand. I will work, and none shall hinder." Tarry out our post of watching our own soul is tarrying at Jerusalem. The result is spiritual radiance, equal to spreading healing and inspiring works around the globe. "Go ye unto all the world and teach, beginning at Jerusalem!"

This is the straight opposite to the urging of martyrs to "come up to the help of the Lord against the mighty." By true understanding we find that the Lord is himself the only mighty one, and needs no help. What a rest for the weary religionists is the doctrine that man is relieved of responsibility for the inspiration of the world. While he is watching his own soul, it is using him for transforming the universe. It is casting the spell of heaven over the hurrying crowds of time and without oratory or pompous endeavor soul has won the soul of man from zone to zone.

The Church that has known enough to select the winners from among those who could cast spells has been feebly imitating the true ministry of the Holy Ghost through the conniving ministers who have learned to tarry at Jerusalem till endued with power.

There are thirteen stars of meaning shining through the last thirteen lessons. They are not stars which ordinary telescopes reveal, but are plain on the sensitized plate of a clear mind that lets the faith of Jesus Christ be faith enough, and lets the soul do its own handling of this world.

The lesson on June 16 taught that the mind that knows better than to swing its thoughts up and down and around about will find all heaven printing its brilliant wisdom on its limpid surface. It was symbolized by Peter, who leaped naked into the sea and received the heavenly injunctions.

<u>Review of Lessons for Weeks Past</u>

June 9 taught that there is an indwelling light in every man which teaches him how to stop going with its hands and tongue and feet in the directions he is now proceeding and teaches him to walk and talk and touch along the beautiful paths of the country that lies nigh that our faces stroke its balmy ethers every move we make.

June 2 taught that every man must find heaven for himself before he is safe pilot over life's roaring main for his neighbors. The standing illustration of stretching ourselves to give what we haven't got and lead toward a heaven we haven't ourselves proved, is the leaning tower of Pisa. When man has found the heaven he is struggling to steer his neighbors into he will never attempt any he cannot instantly accomplish and nobody will ever ask him for anything he cannot instantly give.

May 26 taught that when we hear the people crying out that they do not know what to believe we may know that this is Jesus giving up the ghost. To give up the ghostly place where we do our thinking is the last act before the thinkless soul within us confers upon its dominion over nature with ability to lay down our body and take it up at will.

May 19 taught that the greatness of Jesus was that while he knew that by the swing of one thought he could lay Pilate and all the Roman soldiers low, he did nothing but let each man see an image of himself on the clear, still surface of mind. He took the criminality of the whole world and held it so still that forever after any man who sees a criminal in his brother man shall be only seeing an image of his own self as in a mirror. *Ecce homo* (Behold the man). The jealous man sees a rival, the numerous man sees an enemy, the coward sees a coward. There are no criminals only as we feel criminality. There are no paupers only as we have poor opinions. On the clear surface off the everywhere present sinless man what do we see?

May 12 taught that while we are in the world we do not have to do as the world does and yet we have all the prospering protection which the world is jumping around after. It teaches that we have no need to use our thoughts to manage our destinies with any more than to use our hands. Both are external clatter flourishing around as windmills to keep the central judgment from shining forth.

What We Have Been Learning

May 5 taught that it is mental thralldom to be clinging to human beings for confirmation of our wonderfulness and for sympathy in our undertakings. Jesus clung once and let go once and became the prophesied free handful of corn on the mountain top of supreme isolation that acquaintance with him might forever mean self-supporting, self-inspiring "me," everywhere, in all mankind.

April 28 showed that intellect is the keeper of the thoughts that scamper and fly and falter and rot according to the subject it picks for them to handle. They tire easily and get lost easily and poor intellect, even in our Ruskins and Emersons, gets so harried and bedraggled that it is good for nothing. Judas symbolized the intellect at its everlasting trick of reasoning out from postulates and premises. He finally hanged himself and after that the twelve disciples amounted to something worthwhile. Man will never see his twelve powers spread their glorious spell over lands and seas till he stops letting his intellect have so much to say. There is a spirit in man and the inspiration of the everlasting and all powerful is in its breath.

April 21 taught that the principle we have committed our mind to is our Lord. It will come upon us suddenly some day and saw us asunder. If we have it for our principle that we must work or starve we shall be crying around the syndicate's office windows with empty dinner pails begging them to give us work that we may not have to die. If we have it as a principle that the Lord will always provide for us whether the corporations open their spool factories or not, it is to the eternal glory of that principle that we shall always be independent of convictions.

Strength Which Comes of Knowledge

April 14 had it clearly stated that when we know the majestic "I am" at our center we are not affected by our thoughts and spoken words either by their making us sick if we talk of sickness or well if we talk of wholeness. We can handle thoughts and speech without their unbalancing us from our poised place. As Jesus called himself a rejected stone and a defeated self one moment and the unconquerable son of the Absolute the next moment without affecting his health or his ownership of the universe.

April 7 exposed that when the Christian doctrine is actually told we shall find the children of the world rushing out of the factories, the mines, the stores, and singing hosannas to the name of the highest. It is the opposite of Christianity that shuts them up and no boasting of the triumphs of civilization can hide this fact. It taught that it shall not be for any man's works that he shall hear the songs of Zion chanting his praise and find the world's open doors bidding him welcome. But for finding his own name and remembering the kingship with which he was vested in the royal home whence he came forth. For if the telescope of the intellect at its topmost have never caught the fact that the poorhouse baby is of the royal house of Zion the sensitized plate of a mind that has dropped all the teachings of earth that heavenly secrets may print their eternal virtues on its surface can fearlessly declare that the little one's gleaming spirit is now reigning monarch over worlds and on worlds endless and splendid.

The Chicago Inter Ocean Newspaper, June 30, 1895

Notes

Other Books by Emma Curtis Hopkins

- *Class Lessons of 1888 (WiseWoman Press)*
- *Bible Interpretations (WiseWoman Press)*
- *First Lessons in Christian Science (Desert Church of the Learning Light)*
- *Esoteric Philosophy in Spiritual Science (WiseWoman Press)*
- *Genesis Series 1894 (WiseWoman Press)*
- *High Mysticism (WiseWoman Press)*
- *Self Treatments with Radiant I Am (WiseWoman Press)*
- *The Gospel Series (WiseWoman Press)*
- *Judgment Series in Spiritual Science (WiseWoman Press)*
- *Drops of Gold (WiseWoman Press)*
- *Resume (WiseWoman Press)*
- *Scientific Christian Mental Practice (DeVorss)*

Books about Emma Curtis Hopkins and her teachings

- *Emma Curtis Hopkins, Forgotten Founder of New Thought –* Gail Harley
- *Unveiling Your Hidden Power: Emma Curtis Hopkins' Metaphysics for the 21st Century (also as a Workbook and as A Guide for Teachers) – Ruth L. Miller*
- *Power to Heal: Easy reading biography for all ages –Ruth Miller*

To find more of Emma's work, including some previously unpublished material, log on to:

www.highwatch.org

www.emmacurtishopkins.com

WISEWOMAN PRESS

Vancouver, WA 98665
800.603.3005
www.wisewomanpress.com

Books Published by WiseWoman Press

By Emma Curtis Hopkins

- *Resume*
- *The Gospel Series*
- *Genesis Series 1894*
- *Class Lessons of 1888*
- *Self Treatments including Radiant I Am*
- *High Mysticism*
- *Esoteric Philosophy in Spiritual Science*
- *Drops of Gold Journal*
- *Judgment Series*
- *Bible Interpretations: Series I, thru XXII*

By Ruth L. Miller

- *Unveiling Your Hidden Power: Emma Curtis Hopkins' Metaphysics for the 21st Century*
- *Coming into Freedom: Emily Cady's Lessons in Truth for the 21st Century*
- *150 Years of Healing: The Founders and Science of New Thought*
- *Power Beyond Magic: Ernest Holmes Biography*
- *Power to Heal: Emma Curtis Hopkins Biography*
- *The Power of Unity: Charles Fillmore Biography*
- *Power of Thought: Phineas P. Quimby Biography*
- *The Power of Insight: Thomas Troward Biography*
- *Gracie's Adventures with God*
- *Uncommon Prayer*
- *Spiritual Success*
- *Finding the Path*

www.wisewomanpress.com

List of
Bible Interpretation Series,
with dates,
from
the First - the Twenty-second
Series

This list is complete through the twenty second Series. Emma produced twenty-eight *Series* of *Bible Interpretations.*

She followed the Bible Passages provided by the International Committee of Clerics who produced the Bible Quotations for each year's use in churches all over the world.

Emma used these for her column of Bible Interpretations in both the *Christian Science Magazine,* at her Seminary and in the *Chicago Inter-Ocean Newspaper.*

First Series

July 5 - September 27, 1891

Second Series

Third Series

January 3 - March 27, 1892

Fourth Series

April 3 - June 26, 1892

Lesson 1	Realm of Thought	April 3rd
	Psalm 1:1-6	
Lesson 2	The Power of Faith	April 10th
	Psalm 2:1- 12	
Lesson 3	Let the Spirit Work	April 17th
	Psalm 19:1-14	
Lesson 4	Christ is Dominion	April 24th
	Psalm 23:1-6	
Lesson 5	External or Mystic	May 1st
	Psalm 51:1-13	
Lesson 6	Value of Early Beliefs	May 8th
	Psalm 72: 1-9	
Lesson 7	Truth Makes Free	May 15th
	Psalm 84:1- 12	
Lesson 8	False Ideas of God	May 22nd
	Psalm 103:1-22	
Lesson 9	But Men Must Work	May 29th
	Daniel 1:8-21	
Lesson 10	Artificial Helps	June 5th
	Daniel 2:36-49	
Lesson 11	Dwelling in Perfect Life	June 12th
	Daniel 3:13-25	
Lesson 12	Which Streak Shall Rule	June 19th
	Daniel 6:16-28	
Lesson 13	See Things as They Are	June 26th
	Review of 12 Lessons	

Fifth Series

July 3 - September 18, 1892

Sixth Series

Seventh Series

January 1 - March 31, 1893

Eighth Series

April 2 - June 25, 1893

Lesson 1	The Resurrection of Christ *Matthew 28:1-10*	April 2nd
Lesson 2	Universal Energy *Book of Job, Part 1*	April 9th
Lesson 3	Strength From Confidence *Book of Job, Part II*	April 16th
Lesson 4	The New Doctrine Brought Out *Book of Job, Part III*	April 23rd
Lesson 5	Wisdom's Warning *Proverbs 1:20-23*	April 30th
Lesson 6	The Law of Understanding *Proverbs 3*	May 7th
Lesson 7	Self-Esteem *Proverbs 12:1-15*	May 14th
Lesson 8	Physical vs. Spiritual Power *Proverbs 23:29-35*	May 21st
Lesson 9	Only One Power (information taken from Review)	May 28th
Lesson 10	Recognizing Our Spiritual Nature *Proverbs 31:10-31*	June 4th
Lesson 11	Intuition *Ezekiel 8:2-3, Ezekiel 9:3-6, 11*	June 11th
Lesson 12	The Power of Faith *Malachi*	June 18th
Lesson 13	Review of the 2nd Quarter *Proverbs 31:10-31*	June 25th

Ninth Series

July 2 - September 27, 1893

Lesson 1	Secret of all Power *Acts 16: 6-15*	July 2nd
Lesson 2	The Flame of Spiritual Verity *Acts 16:18*	July 9th
Lesson 3	Healing Energy Gifts *Acts 18:19-21*	July 16th
Lesson 4	Be Still My Soul *Acts 17:16-24*	July 23rd
Lesson 5	(Missing) Acts 18:1-11	July 30th
Lesson 6	Missing No Lesson *	August 6th
Lesson 7	The Comforter is the Holy Ghost *Acts 20*	August 13th
Lesson 8	Conscious of a Lofty Purpose *Acts 21*	August 20th
Lesson 9	Measure of Understanding *Acts 24:19-32*	August 27th
Lesson 10	The Angels of Paul *Acts 23:25-26*	September 3rd
Lesson 11	The Hope of Israel *Acts 28:20-31*	September 10th
Lesson 12	Joy in the Holy Ghost *Romans 14*	September 17th
Lesson 13	Review *Acts 26-19-32*	September 24th

Tenth Series

Eleventh Series

January 1 – March 25, 1894

Twelfth Series

April 1 – June 24, 1894

Thirteenth Series

July 1 – September 30, 1894

Fourteenth Series

October 7 – December 30, 1894

Fifteenth Series

January 6-March 31, 1895

Sixteenth Series

April 7-June 30, 1895

Lesson 1	The Triumphal Entry *Mark 11:1-11*	April 7th
Lesson 2	The Easter Lesson *Mark 12:1-12*	April 14th
Lesson 3	Watchfulness Mark 24:42-51	April 21st
Lesson 4	The Lord's Supper *Mark 14:12-26*	April 28th
Lesson 5	Jesus in Gethsemane Mark 15:42-52	May 5th
Lesson 6	The Jesus Christ Power *Mark 14:53-72*	May 12th
Lesson 7	Jesus Before Pilate *Mark 15:1-15*	May 19th
Lesson 8	The Day of the Crucifixion *Mark 15:22-37*	May 26th
Lesson 9	At the Tomb *Mark 16:1-8*	June 2nd
Lesson 10	The Road To Emmaus *Luke 24:13-32*	June 9th
Lesson 11	Fisher of Men *John 21:4-17*	June 16th
Lesson 12	Missing Luke 24:27-29	June 23rd
Lesson 13	Review	June 30th

Seventeenth Series

July 7 – September 29, 1895

CPSIA information can be obtained
at www.ICGtesting.com
Printed in the USA
LVOW13s2157300317
529125LV00010B/667/P